MASTER CRITICAL THINKING, CREATIVE, LOGIC & PROBLEM SOLVING SKILLS

4 Books in 1

Develop Deep Thinking Skills to Make Smarter
Decisions and Solve Problems in Any Situation

ʻ

By

William Henderson

Content

Book# 1

A Guide to Critical Thinking

Learn How to Take Charge of Your Mind and Make Better Decisions

Introduction

There is a powerful force that shapes all our lives. That force may determine whether we live a life of success and fulfillment or scarcity and desperation. This force is expressed by us daily, innumerable times. The force I am speaking of is our decisions.

With each decision you make, you are putting a cause into motion. In turn, that cause leads to an effect. The effects of your decisions impact all aspects of your life. It is like tossing a pebble into a pond. That single pebble will send ripples that spread in all directions.

Ultimately, every decision we make is to minimize the consequences and maximize the benefits to ourselves or those around us. For this reason, **our decisions function as a cost-benefit analysis for:**

- Our emotional well-being

- Our physical well-being

- The well-being of our relationships

- Our financial well-being

- Our material life

In turn, the quality of our decisions is determined by the quality of our thinking. The decisions we make can be based on fear or ignorance, or they can be based on critical thinking.

When we base our decisions on fear or ignorance, we experience the effects in our personal lives. And when our collective decisions are based on fear or ignorance, we experience the effects at a societal and global level.

The alternative to basing our decisions on fear and ignorance is to base them on critical thinking.

When we think critically, we become aware of how we are making our decisions. Our decisions come from clarity and wisdom rather than fear or ignorance. A lack of critical thinking is behind the political divide we face in this country, the environmental issues we face, our response to the COVID-19 epidemic, and many other challenges.

Critical thinking is not something we are born with. Rather, it is a skill that all of us can learn, which is why I wrote this book. Our individual and collective interests need to develop our critical thinking skills. Doing so can create greater happiness for yourself and contribute to a better world.

CHAPTER 1

Foundations of Critical Thinking

Before discussing the foundations of critical thinking, I would like to share with you an example of why we need critical thinking more than ever:

The COVID-19 virus originated in Wuhan, China, and the first recorded person to become infected was on November 17, 2019. However, it was not until January 23, 2020, that Wuhan implemented strict control (Kuo, 2020).

The first case of infection in the United States was on January 20, 2020. On January 31, Washington implemented a travel ban on Chinese foreign nationals from entering the United States, with a few exceptions (Scripps National, 2023).

However, the ban did not consider the estimated 400,000 travelers from China who arrived in the United States after the beginning of Wuhan's outbreak and before the travel ban was implemented (News 18, 2020). It also did not consider the estimated five million people who entered the United States before Wuhan's strict quarantine measures.

Late January 2020, it was noted by China's National Health Commission that infected individuals posed a threat of spreading the virus. However, the Centers for Disease Control and Prevention announced that it had no evidence of this (Zanin et al., 2020).

These dramatic examples demonstrate why learning critical thinking is so important. In some situations, it is not enough to observe, assess, and adjust one's responses. There is a need for an analysis that is more thoughtful.

Further, the epidemic demonstrated how the traditional leadership model is not adequate. True leadership involves choosing to do the right thing over being right. Our response to the pandemic clearly shows the urgent need for critical thinking.

What is Critical Thinking?

Critical thinking involves learning to guide your decision-making by collecting, analyzing, and evaluating information. Critical thinking is about using reason to guide your decisions. Additionally, critical thinking involves questioning each step in your thought process.

Developing critical thinking skills allows you to think rationally and critically when responding to a situation. When you think critically, you can look beyond the face value of a situation. In doing so, you will gain insight into situations that others overlook.

Thinking critically also involves understanding the connection between multiple concepts.

Let's use a company's example to better understand what critical thinking entails. The company is working on developing a pricing strategy for its product. Involved in this effort are the company's marketing and sales departments.

These departments must work together in a coordinated effort to analyze ways to maximize sales. However, they also must support the company's profit goals. The only viable decision recognizes the connection between marketing and sales.

The following are examples of critical thinking:

- A person experiences their friend's anger who is emotional. Though the friend makes snide comments to them, the person tries to find ways to support them.

- A manager attempts to remain objective while resolving a dispute by listening to both sides and coming up with alternative solutions to the conflict.

- A group of researchers collaborate on a complex project to gather and analyze the data.

- A writer develops ideas for a story's plot while considering the complex motives of the story's characters.

- A small business owner explores his business strategies' potential economic and human consequences to reduce costs and increase income.

- A sports team coach uses halftime to discuss ways to gain an advantage over the opposing team with his players.

- A first responder arrives at an emergency and proceeds to analyze the scene, determine the priorities, and determine what actions are needed and the order of their execution.

- A job applicant preparing for an interview rehearses their responses to highlight their qualifications in a way that is relevant to the employer's needs.

- Parents start planning for their young child's college education by analyzing their projected income and preparing a budget so they can save up to cover this expense.

- A teacher uses questioning to guide their students to develop new insights.

These everyday examples of critical thinking share one thing in common. In each case, the person takes information and uses logic to analyze it carefully. This is different from creative thinking, which involves developing original ideas. When you combine critical and creative thinking, you will maximize the outcome of any situation.

The Ingredients of Critical Thinking

If critical thinking were a fancy dish, it would have the following five ingredients:

Character Traits

The following are the character traits of critical thinkers. Though some of these character traits may be inherited, most can be developed through practice.

- Open-mindedness.

- Acknowledging the evidence.

- Being able to consider different perspectives or points of view.

- Not restricting yourself to any one position.

- Having a healthy skepticism.

- The ability to seek clarity.

Constructive Conflict

Those who are critical thinkers engage in constructive conflict with others and themselves. While conflict normally carries negative associations with it, constructive conflict is positive. **Constructive conflict has the following characteristics:**

- It results in conflicting parties developing new ideas or perspectives.

- The effects of the conflict include increased collaboration and engagement.

- It leads to greater clarity or a reassessment of the situation.

- It improves interpersonal relations (Wolfe, 2021).

Reasoning

Critical thinking also involves drawing conclusions. It requires looking at the facts and the arguments presented and using reason to come up with a logical conclusion.

Discernment

Part of critical thinking is learning to discern truths from untruths. The information we receive will likely vary as to how accurate it is. It is important to use discernment to determine if your information is believable.

Metacognition

Metacognition has to do with the ability to examine your own thinking. It is the ability to examine your thinking patterns to determine if any biases exist, if any aspects of a situation were overlooked, or if there are other flaws. By being able to do this, you will come up with a more accurate conclusion.

The Stages of Critical Thinking

Now that we have explored the nature of critical thinking, we can move on to understanding its stages of development. The stage theory of critical thinking was developed by psychologists (Big Think, 2020).

By understanding the stages of development, you will be able to identify the stage you are at and the direction you can take to reach the next level. The ability to move up in stages depends on your commitment to developing the abilities needed for each stage. We will begin with the lowest stage of critical thinking and move upward (Big Think, 2020).

Unreflective Thinker

Those at this stage of critical thinking do not reflect on their thinking or how it affects their lives. Their opinions and decisions are founded on misconceptions and prejudices. At this level, the skills to parse their thought process are underdeveloped. Additionally, they do not consistently use logic, relevance, or accuracy standards. It is important to note that this level of critical thinking can exist regardless of your educational background (Big Think, 2020).

Challenged Thinker

The challenged thinker is like the unreflective thinker, except for one significant difference. The challenger thinker is self-aware in that they realize the importance of quality thinking and its effect on their lives by not developing this ability.

The person who is a challenged thinker realizes that being a critical thinker requires reflective thinking. They can also recognize the flaws in their own thinking, though they may not be able to identify them (Big Think, 2020).

The biggest challenge for those at this level is that they may have difficulty believing that they have the potential to develop their thinking further. In other words, they feel that they are stuck with their thinking process.

Beginning Thinker

One of the characteristics of the beginning thinker stage is that you become more self-aware. Also, your thinking aligns more with reason. You also begin to recognize the concepts and biases that form the basis of your thoughts (Big Think, 2020).

Beginning thinkers also develop standards regarding how information aligns with logic, accuracy, and clarity. They also have an awareness of how their ego can affect their thinking. They may still have difficulty forming viable solutions to problems at this stage. Lastly, this stage also marks the beginning of being able to accept criticism (Big Think, 2020).

Practicing Thinker

The practicing thinker stage is characterized by the ability to recognize the deficiencies in your thinking process and the skills to manage those deficiencies. At this stage, you can analyze your thinking process and intentionally work on developing your mental skills regularly.

At this stage, you are still vulnerable to giving in to your ego and self-deception (Big Think, 2020).

Advanced Thinker

At the advanced thinker stage, you are effective at being self-critical of your thoughts and finding ways to improve your thinking process. (Big Think, 2020). You can also break out of your repetitive thinking patterns and find new perspectives. You can also practice intellectual integrity, where you can spot the contradictions and inconsistencies in your life. (Big Think, 2020).

Intellectual empathy is another hallmark of this stage, where you can put yourself in other people's situations. Lastly, you have intellectual courage to confront your negative beliefs that no longer serve you (Big Think, 2020).

Master Thinker

At the master thinker stage, you are in total control over how you make decisions and process information. You begin gaining control of your ego, consistently developing your mental skills, and raising your awareness. At the same time, you continuously reexamine your assumptions for weaknesses or biases (Big Think, 2020).

CHAPTER 2

Developing Critical Thinking Skills

In Chapter 1, we discussed the nature of critical thinking. In this chapter, we will explore the different factors that lead to flaws in our thinking. We will begin with cognitive biases and logical fallacies.

Identifying Cognitive Bias

Cognitive bias refers to an error in the way that we process information. This error occurs due to the way our brains work. We all experience cognitive bias, and it is important to understand it. These errors in our thinking may lead us to make decisions based on flawed thinking.

Our brains need to process a great deal of information. To handle all that information, the brain tries to find shortcuts in the way that it processes it. These shortcuts are necessary for us to make quick decisions related to our experiences in the world. Let's say you are walking across the street when you notice an approaching car that does not appear to slow down. Making sense of what is happening at that moment and deciding how you will respond requires quick thinking. You do not have time to contemplate how to respond to that situation.

However, these mental shortcuts are not the only causes of cognitive bias. Cognitive bias can also be the result of our memories. How you remember things may be inaccurate, thus biased. In turn, these inaccurate memories may lead to flawed thinking and decision-making.

Another way cognitive bias can occur is through our attention. We can only pay attention to some things at a time. Because of this, we pay selective attention. We only pay attention to specific aspects of our experience. **The following are examples of cognitive bias:**

- A person limits their attention to new stories that are consistent with their opinion.

- A person blames others when things do not go their way.

- A person attributes the success of others to good luck but attributes their own success to their own efforts.

- A person believes that everyone else has the same beliefs and opinions as they do.

- A person starts learning about a subject and then assumes they know everything about it.

When we make judgments about the world around us, we may believe that we are being objective and logical. We may believe that we can take in and evaluate all the available information. In truth, we are often biased in our judgments. In turn, this can lead to faulty decisions that we may act upon.

Cognitive Bias Types

The following are the most common forms of cognitive bias:

Actor-Observer Bias

This kind of bias reveals itself in the tendency to attribute your circumstances to causes outside yourself while attributing others' circumstances to inner causes. An example of this would be attributing your weight issues to genetics, while the weight issues of others are attributed to unhealthy eating habits.

Anchoring Bias

This kind of bias reveals itself when you place too much emphasis on the first information that you learn about. An example of this is when you learn the average price of a product. Without further research, you happen to find the product offered at a lower price. Because of this, you believe that it is a good deal. If you do further research, you may find even better deals.

When our comparisons are restricted to the original information we learned, we cannot make an informed decision.

Attention Bias

Attention bias is when we pay attention to certain things while ignoring others. An example is when someone is interested in buying a specific car. They focus on the car's look and the feel of the drive, but they ignore the car's reviews or mileage.

Availability Heuristic

This form of bias occurs when we focus more on events due to their vividness and recency. An example is when you hear a story about a plane crash on the news. This causes you to avoid flying when the number of car accidents far exceeds the number of plane crashes each year.

Confirmation Bias

Confirmation bias occurs when a person pays attention to information confirming their beliefs while dismissing information contradicting them. A person who believes politicians are crooked will be attracted to new stories that reflect this. On the other hand, positive stories about politicians may be viewed with skepticism.

False Consensus Effect

With the false consensus effect, a person will tend to overestimate the degree to which others agree. A politician may believe that his constituents are against abortion when most of them may believe there should be some exceptions when abortion is allowed.

Functional Fixedness

With this kind of cognitive bias, the person has a one-dimensional view of things. **The following are examples of this:**

- They may believe that people who are homeless do not work when, in fact, there are homeless individuals who do have jobs.

- They may believe that a subordinate at work can only do their assigned job when that person has leadership skills.

- They may believe that to do a certain task, they need a specific tool when there may be other options they could use.

Halo Effect

The halo effect occurs when you allow your overall impressions of a person to determine their thoughts and feelings. A common example is that when you see an attractive person, you may attribute other positive qualities to them. For example, I may see an attractive woman and think her personal and professional life is also positive.

Misinformation Effect

This cognitive bias occurs when we let information alter our memories. Let's say I witnessed a car accident between a red car and a black car. Because the accident occurred so suddenly, I did not see how it occurred or who was at fault. After the accident, someone who knew the driver of the red car told me that the driver had a habit of speeding. That information may alter my memory of the accident, and I will incorporate that information into my memory. I will believe that the driver of the red car was at fault because they were speeding.

Optimism Bias

This cognitive bias leads us to believe that we are more likely to experience success and less likely to experience misfortune than our peers. An example is a person who believes they are less likely to suffer health issues and more likely to live a long life than others because of how they live.

Self-Serving Bias

With this bias, we tend to blame external forces when we experience misfortune but credit ourselves when we experience good fortune. An example of this is gambling. If we are on a winning streak, we may attribute that to our abilities. If we lose, we may attribute it to the odds being stacked against us.

The Dunning-Kruger Effect

This cognitive bias causes us to overestimate our intelligence and capability. It prevents us from recognizing our incompetence. Because I am educated and accomplished, I will focus on this while overlooking my many deficiencies.

Again, we all have degrees of these cognitive biases. When we recognize them, we can manage them. If we do not recognize them, it may lead to decision-making that we will later regret.

In the next section, we will look at logical fallacies.

Identifying Logical Fallacies

Oddly, you have heard someone make statements or arguments as though they were facts. This may have left you questioning the validity of what was said. Odds are, what you heard was a logical fallacy. **Here is an example of a logical fallacy:**

- Healthy people eat a nutritious diet and exercise regularly.

- James eats a nutritious diet and exercises regularly.

- Therefore, James is healthy.

The conclusion that James is healthy is a logical fallacy. I say this because if we dig deeper into this thinking, we will find potential weaknesses in this conclusion. **Here are some examples:**

- James may be unhealthy, but has recently adopted a nutritious diet and is exercising regularly.

- James has lived a healthy lifestyle to help manage a health issue.

- James may live a healthy lifestyle but has a health issue he is unaware of.

Logical fallacies are statements or arguments that are based on flawed reasoning. Logical fallacies can be exposed by challenging them with logic. It is important to confront logical fallacies because others frequently use them to persuade us to believe what they want us to believe. This is the biggest difference between logical fallacies and cognitive bias.

Cognitive biases are usually made unintentionally; they are often unconscious ways of thinking. Logical fallacies are either intentional or adopted out of naivete. A person may use logical fallacies to influence the thinking of others, or they may accept this kind of thinking as fact without questioning it. **The following are common forms of logical fallacies:**

Appeal to Authority

An appeal to authority occurs when you rely on an "expert" source as the basis of your opinion. Even if your source is an expert in their field, that does not necessarily mean their opinion is correct. When relying on expert opinion, you may have misunderstood them, taken them out of context, or been unaware of certain factors undermining your argument. For this reason, do not rely on a single source for your information.

False Inductions

False inductions occur when you confuse correlation with causation. In other words, just because something happened before something else occurred does not mean a causal relationship exists between the two. Let's say that your employer tells their employees they can start listening to music. A month later, your employer informs everyone that the company's performance has increased since allowing employees to listen to music as they work. The ability to listen to music and the company's improved performance do not mean the increase in performance was caused by allowing music to be played. Without further study, these two things are just correlated with each other.

Here is another example: You start changing your eating habits by eating healthier. Soon after changing your diet, you notice you have more energy. While it is true that eating healthier may make you feel more energized, other factors may contribute to you feeling more energized. Perhaps you are getting more sleep or have recovered from a health problem you did not know you were experiencing. Unless you further investigate this, the relationship between your diet changes and how you feel is a correlation rather than causation.

The Slippery Slope

This form of logical fallacy occurs when we use worst-case scenarios to predict the future. **The following are examples of such thinking:**

An employer is reluctant to let certain employees work from home. They are concerned that if they let a few employees work from home, all employees will want to do the same.

A child's parents do not want them to watch a television program while eating dinner. The parents fear that if they allow it, the child will always want to watch television during dinnertime.

A coworker chooses not to lend money to another coworker. The coworker is concerned that if they lend money to them, that person will always turn to them when they need money.

The Bandwagon Fallacy

This logical fallacy operates on the perception that if many people support an idea or belief, then it must be good, so we buy into it as well. It is not difficult to go back in history to find examples of how a thought or idea that gained popularity resulted in regret, for example, in the fashion and music industries.

The fact that many people agree with or support something does not make it true or the right thing to do. Let's use an example of a store owner who surveys their customers on the idea of the store staying open twenty-four hours a day. The survey shows that customers like the idea. The store owner starts working on a schedule for employees to ensure coverage over twenty-four hours.

The flaw in the thinking of the store owner is that they did not follow up on the survey with additional research. For example, who were the customers that were surveyed? Would these customers actually make a purchase in the early morning hours? If they indicate that they would make a purchase, how often would they do so? What would be the costs of running a store twenty-four hours a day?

Do not rely on your impressions of what the masses would do when making an important decision. You need to back up your impression with in-depth research and planning to determine if the benefits of the idea outweigh the costs.

The False Dichotomy Fallacy

Do you ever get presented with a binary decision? You know, when we are forced to choose between two options, phrased as "Either you do this, or you do that?" In many situations such as this, neither option may be the right decision for you.

However, when someone phrases their argument to you as "either or," you may fall for one of the suggested options. By exploring the situation more deeply, you may find alternative options.

Here is an example:

You visit a car dealer because you need a new car. Because of your limited income, you cannot pay for the car outright. The dealer suggests that you purchase the car using their payment plan. Their argument leaves you believing you only have two choices: accept the payment plan or go without a car. If you take time to consider the manner, **you may find other options such as:**

- Use public transportation.

- Save up money to buy a car from a private seller.

- Take out a low-interest loan to purchase a car from a private seller and pay back the lender as quickly as possible.

- Ride a bicycle.

The Straw Man Fallacy

The Straw Man Fallacy involves someone making a false argument to you and then misrepresenting your opposing position. In doing so, they hope to make their argument stronger. **Here is an example:**

A politician wants to propose tightening gun regulations in the district he represents. His interest in making the proposal is to deal with the high incidents of crime and deaths by guns in his community.

A group that opposes the proposal argues that this politician is trying to take away the gun rights of gun owners. Expressing this argument is easier than addressing the problem of crime and gun deaths.

Ways to Deal with Logical Fallacies

To identify a logical fallacy, it is necessary first to understand the basic structure of an argument. Arguments consist of a set of statements where one statement refers to another.

There are two kinds of statements: premises and conclusions. A premise is a statement that provides evidence for the conclusion of an argument. Conclusions are statements that are inferred from the premise. **Here is an example:**

The statement "David does not like eating sour foods" is a premise, as is the statement "Lemons are sour." The conclusion is "David does not like eating lemons."

The premise must completely support the conclusion for an argument to be logical and valid. You can determine this through a two-way approach: deductive and inductive reasoning.

Deductive Reasoning

With deductive reasoning, you begin with a general premise and arrive at a specific conclusion. Here is an example:

Premise 1: Lucky Grocery Store decided to reduce costs by closing its stores in Arizona.

Premise 2: John, an employee of Lucky Grocery Store, is laid off.

Conclusion: John worked at the Lucky Grocery Store in Arizona.

Inductive Reasoning

With inductive reasoning, you begin with a specific premise and then reach a generalized conclusion.

Here is an example:

Premise 1: Lucky Grocery Store notices that for the last five years, its advertising in July increased its sales by an average of 16 percent.

Premise 2: Winter promotions have not increased sales over the same period.

Conclusion: For Lucky Grocery Store to increase sales, it is better to advertise in the summer than in the winter.

Next time you believe you may have been presented with a logical fallacy, test it using these two methods. Try to find flaws in either the premise or the conclusion.

Here is an example:

Premise 1: Lucky Grocery Store decided to reduce costs by closing its stores in Arizona.

Premise 2: John, an employee of Lucky Grocery Store, is laid off.

Conclusion: John worked at the Lucky Grocery Store in Arizona.

The flaw in this example lies in the conclusion. There are various reasons why a company may lay off an employee, and they do not all have to do with reducing costs. For example, there can be a change in job requirements that John may not meet. If this occurred, the layoff could have happened in any state.

Here is another example:

Premise 1: Lucky Grocery Store notices that for the last five years, its advertising in July increased its sales by an average of 16 percent.

Premise 2: Winter promotions have not increased sales over the same period.

Conclusion: For Lucky Grocery Store to increase sales, it is better to advertise in the summer than in the winter.

The problem with this fallacy is that the focus is only on July and winter sales. While it is true that July sales may be better than winter's, are there months that were not mentioned (such as during spring) where sales may have been even better than July's? By providing more complete information, the store could decide better how to spend its advertising dollars.

When presented with what you believe to be a logical fallacy, check for any flaws in the premise or conclusion. If you find any flaws, ask for more evidence.

Information Literacy: Evaluating Sources

There is a saying that you shouldn't believe everything you read. There is a lot of truth behind this statement. So, how do you know if what you are reading is legitimate? One way to do this is to evaluate the sources of what you are reading. Then, you can determine if your reading information is credible.

The first step to evaluating sources is determining the nature of your reading, which takes us to scholarly and popular sources.

Scholarly vs. Popular Sources

Odds are, what you are reading will be either a scholarly or popular source. Scholarly sources are written by researchers whose work has gone through a publication process that includes peer reviews. The work will also likely have a large list of references. These kinds of written works are normally found in academic journals.

On the other hand, popular sources are written for the public. These writings are not subject to peer review and usually do not include a reference list. You generally find popular sources on websites, blogs, magazines, and certain books.

The kind of source you turn to will depend on the kind of information you are looking for. If you want information on whether a certain commercial product has been linked to cancer, you will want to turn to a scholarly source. If, on the other hand, you want to find out about ways to live a healthier lifestyle, you will most likely turn to a popular source.

Primary vs. Secondary Sources

Sources can also be characterized as being primary or secondary. A primary source is written by someone with firsthand experience doing or witnessing the topic being covered. Primary sources include autobiographies, diaries, government documents, news reports written in the field, and even firsthand social media posts.

Secondary sources are removed from the actual event. In other words, they use secondhand information to create their content. Further, they write about the event after it has happened, such as in the case of biographies.

Guidelines for Evaluating Sources

After determining whether the source you need is scholarly, popular, primary, or secondary, the next step is evaluating the source. **The following are some guidelines:**

Check Out the Author

What information can you get about the author? One way to find out is to type the author's name into a search engine. See if you can find out what else they have written or if they have a profile page. You may be able to find out about their educational background.

Start with the Introduction and Preface

When referring to books, start by reading the preface and introduction. Also, check the table of contents to determine what topics will be covered. By doing this, you can gain information about what the author is attempting to accomplish through their writing and whether the book will meet your needs.

Who is the Intended audience?

Browse through the source and pay attention to the writer's vocabulary, style, and tone. Doing this will help you determine who the book is geared toward. Is the content geared to an audience already familiar with the topic, or is it aimed at a general audience?

Opinion, Fact, or Propaganda

The content of a source can normally be classified as opinion, fact, or propaganda. Opinions express the thoughts of the author, while facts are objective truths. Propaganda is biased information that is spread to benefit a specific individual, group, or cause.

The following are examples:

- Fact: President Biden is the president of the United States.

- Opinion: President Biden is too old to be president.

- Propaganda: President Biden is covering up the questionable behaviors of his son, Hunter Biden. For this reason, Biden needs to be impeached.

It should be noted that propaganda also differs from an opinion in that propaganda normally contains a hidden agenda. Also, even if there is an element of truth in propaganda, it is usually distorted or blown out of proportion.

What Language is Being Used?

What kind of language is used in the source? Is it emotional or objective? Objective language stays with the facts, while emotional language attempts to create an emotional response from the reader.

What Is the Evidence?

It is important to evaluate the degree of evidence in the source. If the source is based on an opinion, is there sufficient evidence provided to support that opinion? If the book is fact-based, is there enough evidence to avoid simplifying the topic?

Do Cross-Checking

When you read a source, look for another source that covers your topic and compare the information. Do the two sources support each other, or are there discrepancies in things such as specific facts or dates? Doing this will help you determine the credibility of the sources.

Is It Timely?

When was the source written? Depending on the topic and your intentions for using the information, knowing when the source was written can make a big difference in whether you can rely on its information. A book on anthropology written fifteen years ago will probably contain more current information than a book on digital technology written five years ago.

Problem-Solving and Decision-Making Techniques

When you are working toward achieving your goals, one thing is guaranteed. You are going to encounter problems, and you will have to make decisions. **The following is a systematic technique that can help you with both:**

Step 1: Specifically Define the Problem

1. State the problem. Let's say that my problem is "I am having trouble meeting my living costs."

2. Restate the problem more specifically: "I am having trouble paying my electric and water bills this month. I can only afford to pay one of them."

Step 2: Brainstorm Possible Solutions

Write a list of all possible solutions to the problem. Do not worry about the quality of the solution at this point. Also, allow yourself to be creative at problem-solving at this stage. Whatever comes to mind, write down the solution. Try to make your list fifteen items long.

Step 3: Evaluate Your Options

1. For this step, go through your list of solutions and eliminate the ones that do not seem doable or are undesirable for other reasons.

2. Order the remaining items on your list according to your preferences. Place the most preferable solution on top of your list and the least at the bottom.

3. Go through them item by item and determine each of their advantages and disadvantages.

Step 4: Make a Decision

From your list, decide which solution to use. In addition, also decide on the following, **if relevant to your situation:**

- Decide who will be responsible for executing the solution.

- Decide how the solution will be implemented.

- Decide when the solution will be implemented.

Example: Today, I will contact the electric and water company and ask to make payment arrangements.

Step 5: Execute the Solution

Execute the solution just as you planned.

Step 6: Evaluate the Result

1. Evaluate how effective the solution was.

2. Determine if you need to adjust your plan to address the problem better.

3. If you are dissatisfied with the result, return to Step 2 and repeat the process.

Cultivating Creative Thinking

Some people are naturally creative. For the rest of us, we can cultivate creative thinking. Also, there is a good reason for doing this. By developing your creativity, you can view problems from a unique perspective and come up with creative ways to address them. The ability to do this is valued, especially in the business sector. Employers like creative thinkers because they are more effective in performing their jobs. **The following are ways that you can cultivate creative thinking:**

Become a Reader

When you read a book, you can gain insight into the writer's life experiences. The result is that you can see their world from their perspective. This is why reading can be so beneficial for developing your creativity. Regardless of how busy you are, make reading a priority.

Get Involved with Art

Find an artistic endeavor that you can make a part of your lifestyle. Whether you have artistic talent or not, getting involved with art regularly can play an important role in developing your creativity. If you have any doubts about this, Albert Einstein came up with many of his revolutionary ideas while playing a musical instrument. Getting involved in artistic endeavors activates parts of the brain that may lead to developing your creativity.

Expand Your Social Circle

We tend to associate with others who are like us. Doing this does not provide much space for personal growth. Instead, start associating with others whose personalities differ from yours. By learning about others who have lived a life dramatically different from your own, you will gain a greater perspective on life, which leads to greater creativity.

Take Time to Enjoy Nature

Spending a brief time in nature can reduce stress and calm your mind. However, it is important to leave your electronic devices at home. The idea is to enjoy nature and experience it as an escape from your life's stressors and distractions. You will be more open to experiencing creative thoughts in this state of mind.

Learn to Meditate

When you learn to meditate, you can quiet your mind and experience stillness. Most of our thinking revolves around our past and future. As a result, we are not mindful of the present moment. When meditating, you learn to focus on the present moment, which brings about stillness. It is from this space that your creativity arises.

Get Plenty of Sleep

Not getting enough sleep will prevent you from experiencing your creativity. When we push ourselves to perform, our ability to connect with our creativity is sacrificed. Additionally, not getting enough sleep makes it more difficult to retain information.

Keep in Shape

Exercise will boost your mood, which leads to feeling more confident. When we are confident, we expend less energy on worrying and more on doing the job that needs to be done. Because you are more present, you will more likely experience creative thoughts.

Follow Your Bliss

There is a correlation between happiness and creativity. When we are happy, our mental functions operate from a higher place. In turn, operating from a higher place will lead you to your creativity. What has just been described is often referred to as the "flow state." Try to spend as much time as possible doing what you love.

Become a Risk-Taker

Taking risks can expand your creativity by exposing you to various life experiences. By experiencing more of life, you can apply what you learned to new situations. Also, our fears prevent us from trying new things. By taking risks, you can learn to overcome that fear, which will increase your confidence when considering future risks.

Explain Your Problem to Others

Before you attempt to solve a problem, it is important to have a complete grasp of the nature of the problem. One way you can determine this is to explain to someone else what your problem is. If you can fully explain your problem to others, you probably have a good understanding of what you are dealing with.

Work Backward

Sometimes, we may have a problem to which we apply ourselves with great tenacity. What often happens when we do this is that we experience a mental block or run out of ideas as to how to solve the problem. If you experience this, try working backward instead.

Let's say my problem is that I am trying to write a book; however, I am running out of ideas. Instead of trying to come up with ideas to complete the book, I could imagine that the book was already written.

Working backward, I would identify the character plots that come up as I break down the book.

When I have my plot ideas, I can implement them in my writing. In the next chapter, we will discuss ways that critical thinking is put into practice.

CHAPTER 3

Critical Thinking in Practice

In this chapter, we will explore the role of critical thinking in our everyday lives. We will begin with education.

Critical Thinking in Education

You may find this surprising, but critical thinking is not practiced in public education, which is where you would most expect it to be. You would think that the goal of American public schools would be to teach students how to think critically so that they can think for themselves. The following are some research findings regarding the teaching of critical thinking:

The teaching of critical thinking varies from state to state. Further, the teaching of critical thinking decreases as students get older.

Eighty-six percent of fourth-grade teachers reported that they emphasize teaching deductive thinking skills (a form of critical thinking), but only 39 percent of eighth-grade teachers did so. In a survey of eighth-grade teachers, only seven states indicated that they emphasized deductive reasoning (Taunque, 2022).

Theories as to why the teaching of critical thinking declines when moving up the grade levels may be due to schools needing to meet state accountability standards (Hamilton et al., 2002). In many states, students cannot attend high school if they do not pass standardized state exams. Success on the standardized exams is also tied to school funding and teacher pay.

Because of the pressure to meet performance standards, the focus is on getting students to pass the state exams instead of learning to think critically.

Critical Thinking in the Workplace

Critical thinking skills are becoming increasingly important in today's workplace. Due to technological advancements and a competitive environment, businesses must deal with continuous change. The World Economic Forum announced that by 2025, critical thinking will be the most sought-after skill by employers (Zahidi, 2020). Despite this, few companies provide training in critical thinking.

Employers are looking for employees who can analyze and evaluate information and then make informed decisions based on it. By doing so, they can identify new opportunities or find creative solutions to workplace problems.

Additionally, employees who can think critically can more effectively communicate their ideas to team members, customers, and vendors. Those who can think critically are seen as valuable assets in any business.

Everyday Critical Thinking: Personal and Social Applications

Whether you realize it or not, being able to think critically is essential to living a happy life. Your quality of life is largely shaped by your ability to think critically. The reason for this is quite basic. Our actions are born from the decisions we make. Those actions we continuously repeat become our habits. In turn, our habits shape our destiny.

Let me use my own life as an example of what I mean by this. During the first half of my life, I lacked confidence and self-esteem. I felt inadequate both socially and in my work. For this reason, I had low expectations for myself regarding the life I could live.

This kind of thinking resulted in me taking the easy way out. When it came to my life, I took the path of least resistance. I did not believe I could advance to a successful career, so I did not give it my full effort. I rarely dated because I did not feel confident when I interacted with members of the opposite sex. Because of how I felt about myself, I spent most of my time alone.

These beliefs that I had about myself and the habits that I lived by were shaping my destiny. In my mind, I believed I was condemned to a future of mediocrity and loneliness.

When I reached my early thirties, I experienced a drastic shift in how I saw myself. I had reached a point where I was tired of living the life I was leading. I started focusing all my free time on self-development. I exposed myself to different perspectives as to how my life could be. I also aggressively applied what I learned to my life.

Because I changed my thinking, my actions changed. I started to think about myself and my possibilities differently. I became increasingly self-confident and willing to challenge myself.

These actions became my new habits. In turn, these habits created for me a new destiny. Today, I enjoy a happy marriage and a successful career.

The basis of my life's transformation was that I began to think critically. When I say that I began thinking critically, I do not mean thinking critically in a negative way. Rather, I looked honestly at how I was living my life. I was willing to challenge my limiting assumptions about my life.

When we do not practice critical thinking in our daily lives, we willingly allow our limiting beliefs to define our lives. When we learn to think critically, we can challenge our limiting beliefs and create a new destiny for ourselves.

What makes critical thinking so powerful is that it gets us to be more creative in our thinking. Critical thinking promotes problem-solving and the ability to come up with new ideas. My life changed because I engaged in problem-solving rather than allowing my problems to define my life. My life changed because I allowed myself to think creatively about what I could do with it.

As important as problem-solving and creativity were in changing my life direction, none of that would have occurred if I did not engage in self-reflection. Self-reflection is what fosters critical thinking. In turn, critical thinking fosters self-reflection.

Critical Thinking, Ethical & Social Responsibility

We will begin this section with a look at the delicate balance between critical thinking, ethical considerations, and social responsibility. We will then discuss examples of real-world scenarios where critical thinking is demonstrated.

Ethical & Social Responsibility

If you think of the mind as a tool belt, critical thinking is just one of the tools. Another tool is ethical thinking. To be a true leader, you need both. This is because critical thinking and ethical thinking serve separate functions.

Critical thinking involves decision-making that does not always consider the consequences for others. For example, I could use critical thinking to determine which solution best meets my needs while ignoring the impact on others.

On the other hand, ethical thinking focuses on how our decisions impact others. Thus, critical thinking can conflict with ethical thinking. The mark of a true leader is the one who uses ethical thinking to inform their critical thinking.

It is also important to strike a balance between social responsibility and critical thinking. This is particularly true in the business world. Business is increasingly becoming aware of the importance of corporate social responsibility (CSR).

However, it takes critical thinking to determine how CSR will be demonstrated. Using critical thinking can result in an alignment between a company's CSR efforts and its values. Further, critical thinking can make the implementation of CSR more effective.

If a company wants to reduce its footprint on the environment, critical thinking and CSR would ideally be blended to determine how to do that most effectively while continuing to support the company.

All changes begin from within and are reflected outwardly. Critical thinking is the origin of everything that I enjoy in my life today. We will take a closer look at self-reflection in the next chapter.

CHAPTER 4

Enhancing Critical Thinking Abilities

In this chapter, we will explore some of the elements of critical thinking and how you can further develop them. We will begin with self-reflection.

Self-Reflection

Self-reflection is a component of critical thinking that involves reflecting on your experiences and what you have learned. Engaging in self-reflection can help you improve your ability to make decisions and problem-solve.

You can use self-reflection in problem-solving by doing some reverse engineering. You can find a better solution by breaking down a problem into its most basic parts. **The following are the steps to using self-reflection in problem-solving (Gitt, 2019):**

1. Collect the Data

For this first step, you want to collect as much information as possible regarding the problem you are facing. For example, let's say you are trying to lose weight. The data you collect may consist of keeping a daily record of what you ate and when you ate it. By gathering this data, you can come up with a baseline as to where you are with your eating habits (Gitt, 2019).

After you have analyzed your data, you will be ready for the next step, which is self-reflection.

2. Self-Reflect about the Problem

Schedule an hour when you can self-reflect on the problem. Arrange it so that you will not be disturbed by anyone during this time. During this time, you will be writing. Before explaining the exercise, **keep the following guidelines in mind:**

1. Commit to dedicating the indicated time for each step of the process.

2. Do not worry about grammar, spelling, or format when writing.

3. Do not become distracted as you engage in this process (Gitt, 2019).

Step 1: Break the problem down into smaller pieces.

Time to complete: 15 minutes.

Often, we do not take the time to understand the nature of our problems. For this reason, this first step involves breaking down the problem into its basic pieces. The way to do this is to ask yourself "why" the problem exists. You want to keep asking yourself this question until you can no longer ask it (Gitt, 2019). **The following is an example:**

The problem: I have gained 25 pounds and am concerned about my health.

Ask "why": Why do I have this problem?

Answer: "I am overeating and eating a lot of junk food."

Ask "why": Why do I eat those foods?

Answer: "I do not have healthier foods that I find appealing and filling when I need a snack."

Ask "why": Why do I buy those foods?

Answer: "When I go grocery shopping, I do not prioritize buying healthier foods."

Ask "why": Why do I not prioritize buying healthier foods?

Answer: "I am busy, and I try to rush when I go shopping." (Gitt, 2019.)

By breaking down my problem, I could find the most basic reason for it. I do not prioritize my grocery shopping, so I rush when I do it. Because I rush my shopping, I make purchases out of habit.

Using this process has allowed me to take a complex and undefined problem and clearly define it (Gitt, 2019).

Step 2: Determine why the problem is worth overcoming.

Time to complete: 15 minutes.

At this step, you must reflect on why you must overcome the problem. The reasons that you come up with need to be emotionally compelling for you. To begin this step, take 10 minutes to write down all the reasons why you need to tackle this problem. For this first part, write down whatever comes to mind. **Here is an example:**

Why do I want to lose weight?

1. If I don't lose weight, I increase my risk of a heart attack.

2. Being heavy makes me feel unattractive.

3. I want to feel better about myself.

4. I want to feel healthier.

5. I want to have more energy.

6. I want to look good in my clothes (Gitt, 2019).

This is just a shortlist. Remember to keep writing for ten minutes.

Use the remaining five minutes to prioritize the items on your list. You want to find out which reasons for wanting to change are most important to you (Gitt, 2019).

3. Create a Team

Time to complete: 15 minutes.

In this step, you want to surround yourself with people who can make a difference in overcoming the problem. **To do this, consider the following:**

- Which people are impacted by or connected to this problem? How could they help?

- Who could I turn to as a resource?

- Is there someone I know battling the same problem as I am? Could we team up with each other?

Take ten minutes to write down all the individuals who are connected to the problem. When you have your list, take five minutes to rank those people according to their ability and willingness to assist you. **The following is an example:**

- My spouse can help me with grocery shopping.

- My partner can help me by selecting healthier restaurants to eat at.

- My spouse can help me plan healthier meals (Gitt, 2019).

- My partner can exercise with me.

- A nutritionist can recommend a diet to me.

- My doctor can assess my health (Gitt, 2019).

- My friend can encourage me to eat healthier.

4. Create a Plan

Time to complete: 15 minutes.

To develop your plan, start by stating your goal.

Example: I will lose 25 pounds in six months.

After you have stated your goal, make a list of tasks that you need to complete to reach it. Also, assign a due date for each task on your list. The following is an example:

1. Mark on my calendar the days that I will go grocery shopping. Schedule 40 minutes for each shopping trip. Due: Tomorrow

2. Schedule a doctor's appointment for a physical. Due: April 1

3. Join a health club and enroll in fitness training classes. Due April 2.

4. Find ten recipes for healthy meals that I would enjoy eating. Due April 3.

5. Schedule three exercise sessions per week at my health club. Due: April 4.

Lastly, create a timeline for yourself that reflects when you plan to achieve your goal. Within that timeline, include milestones and interim check-in dates so that you can assess your progress (Gitt, 2019). **Here is an example:**

- My baseline weight is 230 lbs.

- My target weight is 205 lbs.

My check-in points are:

- May 30: The goal is to be 225 1bs.

- June 30: The goal is to be 220 lbs.

- July 30: The goal is to be 215 1bs.

- August 30: The goal is to be 210 lbs.

- September 30: The goal is to be 205 1bs.

5. Feedback

After completing this one-hour exercise, present your plan to two or more people you trust and have some connection to the problem. Ask them for their feedback about our plan. They may be able to point out things that you missed and left out of your plan. Or they may be able to provide you with suggestions that you did not think of.

Socratic Method for Deeper Understanding

A technique that you can use daily to improve your life is the Socratic method.

The Socratic method can help overcome limited or unrealistic thinking. The following are the steps to the Socratic method when used on yourself:

Step 1: Identify your limited or negative thinking:

Example: You have the thought, "I don't know why I should go to the interview. I know I will not get the job."

Step 2: Identify the supporting evidence.

At this step, you look for evidence to support your thinking. You can do this by asking questions.

Example: You have the thought, "I don't know why I should go to the interview. I know I will not get the job."

Ask yourself questions like:

- "What evidence do I have that leads me to believe they will not pick me for the job?"

- "For what reasons do I believe they would disqualify me?"

- "What would be so bad if I was not accepted for the position?

Step 3: Adopt a more empowering perspective.

In Step 2, you asked yourself questions to challenge your thinking. In this step, you will change your perspective by taking on an alternative one.

Example: You have the thought, "I don't know why I should go to the interview. I know I will not get the job."

Alternative perspective: "What do I have to lose by attending the job interview? At worst, I will gain interviewing experience. At best, I will get the position."

Embracing Continuous Learning and Growth

When you adopt a critical thinking mindset, you open yourself up to learning and growth. We live in a dynamic world that is constantly changing. New technologies are constantly being developed, while the world itself is becoming more unpredictable. By continuously learning, you become more adaptable. You put yourself in a better position for opportunities.

Also, continuous learning will lead to greater creativity and innovation. You can use that creativity and innovation to benefit yourself, your family, and your workplace. Finally, continuous learning leads to critical thinking, enabling you to evaluate information more effectively, leading to better decisions.

Real-World Scenarios

In life, there are two kinds of problems: defined and undefined. Defined problems are those that have a clear answer to them. If you have a flat tire, you change the tire. These kinds of problems are routine. However, many problems that we encounter are undefined. An example of an undefined problem is a relationship problem. You may know that your partner is upset with you. However, trying to resolve that upset may lack a clear solution. You may view the problem one way, while your partner views it another way.

One reason that undefined problems can be so challenging is that we often do not have all the relevant information needed to solve the problem. Further, we may be influenced by our egos. For example, we may become defensive in our position and blame the other person for causing the problem. Our biases may also sway us. For these reasons, critical thinking can be used in every aspect of our lives.

By thinking critically, you can make good decisions that make use of the information that you have and avoid your ego or biases. **The following are real-world scenarios that demonstrate the use of critical thinking:**

- A person who is starting a diet throws out all junk food from their pantry to avoid temptation.

- A person working on becoming more time efficient uninstalls the social media apps on their phone to avoid getting distracted.

- A parent places educational toys in the middle of their living room so their child engages with them before playing with their other toys.

- A person creates and schedules his emails to his friends because they do not want to be disrupted while working on a project.

- A person maintains a journal where they write down their ideas to use in the future.

- A person schedules time each day to learn something new as they know how the world is constantly changing.

- A person verbally attacked by another pauses to allow their emotions to settle before replying.

In each of these examples, critical thinking is being demonstrated. It is demonstrated by understanding the current situation and thinking ahead to make the best decision they can.

Conclusion

We are living at a time that is unprecedented in human history. Never has there been a time when we have become so technologically advanced; further, our technology continues to evolve. With this technology comes great responsibility. We have left an indelible mark on our planet. Wars, global warming, and environmental destruction are just some of the existential threats we face.

In our fast-paced society, many of us spend our days glued to our cell phones. Information is so readily available that it can be difficult to decipher what is factual and what is not. These events are just a few of the challenges that we must negotiate. For this reason, the ability to think critically is so badly needed in today's world.

We cannot rely on our governments and leaders to guide us to a better future. These entities are more interested in maintaining political power. For this reason, each of us should learn to think critically. If we can attain a critical mass, we may be able to save our planet.

BOOK 2

How to Make Winning Decisions

A Guide to Problem Solving for All Areas of Your Life

Introduction

What problems are you facing? Are the problems you face today different from those in the past? Looking back at your life, how effective were you at solving your problems? Did your solutions remedy the situation, or did they worsen it? Are there past situations that you wish you had not tried to resolve? Do you feel that you should have gone by the saying, "Let sleeping dogs lie"?

Problems are an inescapable part of life. We all experience them, individually and collectively. There are personal problems, family problems, organizational problems, local problems, national problems, and global problems. Given this fact, you would think that the teaching of problem-solving skills would be a priority for our educational system. Unfortunately, this is not the case.

While it is true that problem solving is incorporated into the curriculum of most educational institutes, there is a failure to teach students how to apply these skills to their daily lives. We may have learned formulas for solving math problems, but most of us have not learned how to use a systematic approach to resolving our personal problems.

Whether it is at the personal or societal level, we experience daily evidence of what happens when we do not utilize problem-solving skills. This evidence can be found in all areas of our lives: emotional, physical, relationships, and finances. When bad decision-making is made by individuals of power and influence, it can have a major impact. **The following are a few examples of bad decision-making on a major scale:**

- In 1977, senior executives at 20th Century Fox agreed to give George Lucas the product merchandising rights to all *Star Wars* movies (Andersen, 2013). In exchange, it was agreed that George Lucas would give Fox Studio a cut of his paycheck in the amount of $20,000. In the end, the combined revenue from product merchandising was more than three billion dollars!

- Coca-Cola decided to change the formulation of its product, which was a century old. The new formulation, New Coke, was introduced to the marketplace in 1985. New Coke lasted 79 days before Coca-Cola returned to its original formulation. The change was made due to public outcry (Becker, 2014).

- In 2014, the governor of Michigan, Rick Snyder, gave power to a select group of people to make drastic changes to their cities' water supply. To save money, the group decided to change the source of the city of Flynt's water supply to the Flint River. The Flint River contained high levels of lead, which caused contamination of the drinking water (Myers, 2019).

- One of the worst decisions in American history was the Vietnam War. The U.S. entered the war with insufficient knowledge of how to fight it. The U.S. presence did little to change anything about the war. The cost of the war was 58,220 American lives, 150,000 wounded, and over $110 billion as of 2013 (Schoppert, 2016).

These are but a few examples of how leaders, despite their intelligence and position, can make major mistakes. These mistakes occurred because they did not understand problem-solving techniques. When you learn problem-solving techniques, you can not only make better decisions for your personal life, but you can also better critique the policy decisions of your leaders.

In this book, you will learn problem-solving techniques to apply to your life. **You will learn the following:**

- **Chapter 1:** The Problem-Solving Mindset.

  Strategies for developing a problem-solving mindset. Learn to become more effective at problem solving.

- **Chapter 2:** Defining the Problem

  How to clearly define the problem. If you do not clearly define the problem, you may be solving the wrong problem.

- **Chapter 3:** Analyzing the Problem

  Different approaches to gain a better understanding of problems.

- **Chapter 4:** Strategic Decision-Making Strategies.

  How to make better decisions and avoid cognitive bias.

- **Chapter 5:** Creative Problem-Solving Techniques.

  How to blend creativity with problem-solving techniques for more innovative solutions.

- **Chapter 6:** Advanced Levels of Problem Solving

  Learn key points for leaders when problem solving.

Learn to take charge of your destiny by learning how to problem solve today!

CHAPTER 1

The Problem-Solving Mindset

In 1958, the Honda motorcycle company found itself being dominated in the U.S. market by its more robust competitors, such as Harley Davidson. Honda later learned that sales of its smaller motorcycles were on the rise. These bikes were being bought by Honda's younger customers who were looking for a form of transportation that was affordable, independent, and convenient.

Realizing this, Honda focused on selling its smaller motorcycles. One year later, Honda went from being a minor player in the market to owning 63 percent of the market share (IED, 2020). Honda's executive team turned around their company by employing a problem-solving mindset.

A mindset is a set of beliefs that dominate one's way of thinking. Our beliefs create our perspective on the world. If I have a set of beliefs that are limiting, I will focus on what is wrong with my life and why I can never get ahead.

If I have a set of empowering beliefs, I will focus on what is possible for my life and the opportunities that are available to me. These are the kinds of beliefs that create a problem-solving mindset.

Characteristics of a Problem-Solving Mindset

To better understand the characteristics of a problem-solving mindset, it is helpful to first look at two types of mindsets: fixed and growth.

Fixed Mindset

Those who have a fixed mindset believe that who they are cannot be changed regarding their characteristics and abilities. Those with this mindset avoid difficult situations and taking risks and are quick to give up when faced with challenges. The reason they behave this way is because they personalize failure. In other words, they see failure as a reflection of their self-worth.

Growth Mindset

A growth mindset is the opposite of a fixed mindset. Those with this mindset believe they can develop their abilities and change their characteristics through learning and practice. They view setbacks as opportunities to better themselves. This is because they do not personalize failure. As a result, they persevere and can overcome their challenges.

Those with a growth mindset tend to also be good at problem solving. While those with a fixed mindset avoid problems, those with a growth mindset view them as opportunities for improvement and growth.

Also, those with a growth mindset view failure differently than those with a fixed mindset. Those with a fixed mindset tend to give up when faced with problems. Because of this, they do not learn from their experience.

Those with a growth mindset see failure as a temporary setback that offers opportunities to learn and improve. By learning from their experience, they become better problem solvers.

How to Change Your Mindset

Fortunately, anyone can change their beliefs and develop a problem-solving mindset. To do so just takes effort and time. The reason for this is the way our brains work. Whenever we learn something new, we change the structure of our brains. The learning of new information causes new neural pathways to be created.

Building new neural pathways requires a great deal of energy. Energy is also needed to override our old ways of doing things and replace them with what we have learned. This is why it takes a concerted effort to change how we are. However, it can be done!

You can do three things to start developing a growth mindset: become curious, dream big, and deal with uncertainty.

1. Become Curious

It is difficult to learn anything if you are uninterested in learning about it! It is for this reason that you should use your interest as a means to develop a growth mindset. Take a moment to think about the things that motivate you. **You can do this by asking yourself questions like:**

- What am I passionate about?

- What do I value?

- How would I like to be as a person?

- How would I like to improve my life?

- What are my goals?

The following are suggestions for what to do when you have identified something that you are curious about:

- Schedule time to think about the topic that you chose. You can do this alone, or you can discuss it with others.

- Do as much research as you can on the topic.

- Expose yourself to others who have an opposing perspective on the topic.

Example: If you are curious about skipping college and getting into the trades, talk to people who believe you should attend college first.

- Talk to others about what they did when faced with an important decision.

- Think back on your past decisions, both successful and unsuccessful. Can you identify any patterns in your thinking that determined whether your decisions were successful? By identifying these patterns, you will know what to look out for when making decisions in the future.

2. Dream Big

By becoming curious, you opened yourself up to gathering information about your topic. Now that you have gathered the information, it is time to dream big. What is it that you would like to achieve ultimately? This is the step where you need to push aside any thoughts of limitation and allow yourself to daydream.

Example: If you are curious about becoming an actor, what would you like your life to be like as an actor?

The following are suggestions for dreaming big:

- Schedule a time when you can focus on your dreams. You can do this alone or with others.

- Talk to or research others who have already walked your path. **Example:** Find out what others did to become actors.

- Think about how you could turn your dreams into reality. What would you have to do? What resources would you need? What would the potential payoffs be for your efforts?

3. Deal with Uncertainty

So far, you have become curious and dreamed big about what you want to achieve. Because planning will be discussed in a later chapter, we will not go into details here. With this in mind, the next step is to deal with uncertainty.

Those with a fixed mindset are bound to allow their fears to hold them back from pursuing their dreams. Dealing with uncertainty will be discussed in more detail in a later chapter; however, **here are some suggestions to get you started:**

- Make sure that you did your research and sought opposing points of view (see the section: *Become Curious*).

- Plan for how you will achieve your goal or dream.

- Develop contingency plans in case your plan does not work out.

Example: If my dream to become a veterinarian does not work out, my contingency plans are:

- o Reapply to a different veterinary college.

- o Find another career that involves working with animals.

- o Get volunteer experience in an animal hospital and then reapply to a veterinary college.

- Understand the pros and cons of your contingency plans.

Example: What would be the pros and cons of reapplying to a different veterinary college?

Doing these three steps will transform your mind from fixed to growth. You will do this by opening yourself to new perspectives and possibilities.

In the next chapter, we will discuss one of the most important steps in problem solving, yet it is often overlooked. I am talking about defining the problem.

CHAPTER 2

Defining the Problem

Years ago, I got married, and we bought a home. My wife decided to start a business, and we were short of money. We decided to refinance and use the money for the business. The business continued to struggle, and we needed more money. Our solution was to refinance again. Five years later, we had to declare bankruptcy.

This period of my life was very painful for my wife and I. I had the added burden of feeling responsible for losing our home. Not understanding the nature of our problems got us into this predicament.

We had not looked deep enough into what was going on with our finances. We had used refinancing as a solution, but that solution only made things worse for us. We chose the wrong solution because we did not understand the nature of our problem. Our problem was that we were trying to live beyond our means. Our problem was that we were trying to support a business with money we did not have.

Just as I did not understand the nature of our problem, neither did Tower Records. Tower Records opened in 1960 in Sacramento, California. By the 1990s, the stores had expanded across the United States and 11 other countries.

The problem was that Tower Records ignored the changes in the music industry, which was shifting to online retailing. It also had a large amount of debt from when it underwent expansion. For these and other reasons, Tower Records went bankrupt in 2006 (DJTees, n.d.).

Before trying to fix a problem, we must first understand the nature of the problem. We need to be able to define and analyze it.

Defining the problem is the first step in problem solving. This step needs to be completed before considering any solutions.

Defining the Problem

Some may think that reading a section on defining problems is not needed. They may say, "I know what the problem is!" I consider myself to be intelligent and well-educated. Yet, my behavior led us to go bankrupt! If you are honest with yourself, I am sure that there were times when your solution to a problem backfired on you. We have all experienced this. The reason why it happens is often due to our not defining the problem that we are dealing with.

When we do not define the problem, we risk making it more difficult to solve. The level of understanding that we have of a problem will determine the quality of the solution and how that solution impacts our lives.

When we correctly define a problem, we can gain insight into why it occurred and resolve it more effectively. One way of defining the problem is to connect to it any goals and barriers that may exist. Doing so will not only define the problem but also identify any subproblems. Here is an example:

My problem: "I need to get to a job interview, but my car has broken down. Also, I do not have the money to get it repaired."

In this case, my goal is to get to my job interview. The first subproblem is that my car broke down. The second subproblem is that I do not have the money to fix it. These subproblems are my barriers. If we separate the goal from the subproblems, we can focus on the immediate problem.

Original problem: "I need to get to my job interview, but my car has broken down. Also, I do not have the money to get it repaired."

The problem defined is: "I need to get to my job interview."

Having defined the problem, I know where to place my focus when it comes to finding a solution. The subproblems can be addressed later. Having defined the problem, you can also determine the problem type that your problem belongs to, which is the topic of the next section.

Problem Types

The Cynefin framework is a classification system that you can use to identify the kind of problem that you are facing. Not only can it identify the problem type, but it also offers suggestions for the kind of solution to look for. The following are the four problem types:

Simple Problem

Simple problems are straightforward, and the solution is obvious. If my tire is flat, I need to replace it. If my lawn is overgrown, I need to mow it. Simple problems have a clear cause-effect relationship. If I replace the tire, I can drive. If I cut the grass, I will have a neat lawn.

Complicated Problems

Unlike simple problems, which are straightforward, complicated problems involve the unknown. You know there is a problem but do not know the answer. When confronted with such a problem, the most common response is to seek out an expert.

I may know that there is something wrong with my dog. I can tell because he is not acting right. But I do not know what is causing him to behave that way. For this reason, I will bring him to the veterinarian.

I may know something is bothering my wife, but I cannot tell what it is. What I can do is ask her about it.

Once you find out what the problem is, you can work on finding a solution. The veterinarian makes a diagnosis and prescribes a treatment. My wife shares what is bothering her, and I do my best to support her.

Complex Problems

Complex problems are those where you do not know what is going on until after the fact. An example is a company that produces a product. They notice that their sales are dropping. The problem is that they do not know why. Is the drop in sales due to inflation and customers cutting back on spending? Is it because recent modifications to the product have not been well received by customers? Is it because there has been a change in trends? The company may not know the answer until time has passed and the company has more information.

When you face a complex problem, it is important that you take some form of action. If your efforts do not improve the situation, try something else. Keep trying out different solutions until you find something that works. When dealing with complex problems, any action you take is better than no action. The reason for this is that each action that you take provides you with feedback. The feedback that you receive is a guide for what to do next.

The company may reduce the price of its product and see if that makes a difference. If this action does not increase sales, it will use that feedback to try something different, and so on. The key is to learn from your feedback and keep trying new things until you get the results you are looking for.

Chaotic Problems

Chaotic problems are considered a crisis or emergency. You do not have time to plan or experiment with different solutions. With chaotic problems, you most likely will not know their cause and effect. Instead, you need to take immediate action in hopes that it will keep the situation from getting worse. You can think about chaotic problems like your house being on fire. There is only one thought that you have: put out the fire!

When you have defined the problem, the next step is to analyze it so that you can get a more complete understanding of it. This is the topic of the next chapter.

CHAPTER 3

Analyzing the Problem

Problem analysis is crucial in problem solving as it allows you to understand the root cause of the problem rather than focusing on the symptoms. The following are ways to conduct problem analysis:

Structuring the Problem

By structuring the problem, you will get a deeper insight into the nature of your problem. Structuring is particularly helpful when dealing with more complex problems.

The first step to structuring the problem is to question it. You want to determine whether your goal is really what you are looking for and if the barriers are really problematic. Or are there other barriers that you overlooked? The second would be looking at the relationships between the problem elements and seeing if you can get further insight into the problem.

We will start with questioning the problem by using the scenario from **Chapter 2:** "I need to get to a job interview, but my car has broken down. Also, I do not have the money to get it repaired.'"

Problem	Questions
"I need to get to my job interview, but my car has broken down. Also, I do not have the money to get it repaired."	• Do I really need this job? • Could I reschedule the interview? • Could I ask the employer if we could do the interview remotely?
	Subproblem 1: • Are there other forms of transportation I could use? • What about public transportation or a taxi?
	Subproblem 2: • Could I sell things to come up with the money? • Would it be cheaper to buy an affordable used vehicle?

While asking questions and challenging your assumptions, you may find other options for addressing your problems. You may find that you do not have a problem at all!

The next step is to look at the relationship between the problem elements. Earlier, **we defined a problem and identified the subproblems:**

The problem defined: "I need to get to my job interview."

Subproblem 1: "My car is broken down."

Subproblem 2: "I have no money."

We can now look at the relationship between these problem elements. In this example, solving any of these three elements will resolve the remaining ones. **For example:**

- If I get to my interview, I may get hired. I would then have the money that I need.

- If I get my car fixed, I can get to the interview.

- If I have money, I can get my car fixed and get to the interview.

By defining and structuring your problem, you can get a deeper understanding of it, allowing you to make better decisions about how you want to address it. The example of the job interview was a clear-cut problem. However, other problems can be far more complex. It is in such situations that defining and analyzing problems can be helpful. Another way to analyze problems is through the 5 Whys method.

The 5 Whys Method

The 5 Whys method involves asking questions to understand the problem better. Using this technique lets you go beyond your assumptions of what is causing the problem and examine it at a deeper level. When you believe you have the answer to a problem, explore it more deeply by asking "WHY" five times as you dig deeper into the answer.

The 5 Whys tool can be used for both personal and business problems. **The following are examples:**

Using "WHY" to Uncover Personal Problems

The problem: I do not call my family often.

1. **Question:** Why do I not call my family often?

   My answer: Because I am busy.

2. **Question:** Why do I not call my family when I have time?

   My answer: Because when I call them, I often feel defensive.

3. **Question:** Why do I feel defensive?

   My answer: Because they tell me how I should live my life.

4. **Question:** Why do I not tell them to stop?

   My Answer: Because I feel like it gets me nowhere.

The root of my problem is not that I am busy. I use that as an excuse for not calling my family often. The root reason is that I have trouble dealing with them. This is the problem that I need to work on.

Here is another personal example:

The problem: I am angry with my partner.

1. **Question:** Why am I angry with my partner?

   My answer: Because she is always late.

2. **Question:** Why does that bother me?

   My answer: Because she does not let me know she will be late.

3. **Question:** Why does that bother me?

   My answer: Because I do not feel like that is being fair to me.

4. **Question:** Why does that bother me?

   My answer: She may not care for me because I feel like that.

As in the previous example, this method allows us to go beyond a superficial understanding of our problems to a more insightful one.

The following is a business example:

The problem: In a manufacturing plant, there has been a drop in production.

1. **Question:** Why has there been a drop in production?

   Answer: Because one of the machines is not working.

2. **Question:** Why is the machine not working?

Answer: Because one of the belts is damaged.

3. **Question:** Why was the belt not repaired?

   Answer: A work order was filed, but we received no response.

4. **Question:** Why was there no response?

   Answer: Because the maintenance department is undergoing contract negotiations.

As you can see, sometimes you can arrive at the root problem by asking "WHY" less than five times. Other times, you may have to ask "WHY" more than five times to get a satisfactory answer.

Root Cause Analysis

Imagine that you are at home when your internet goes down. You have important work to do, so you go to a coffee shop and use their Wi-Fi. You may have found a temporary solution but have not addressed the problem. A more effective solution would have been to contact the internet company to determine the cause.

Unfortunately, we often do something similar when we encounter problems. We fail to address the root cause. This is the purpose of doing a root cause analysis. Performing a root cause analysis will allow you to analyze the sequence of events that led to the problem to determine its cause and what you can do to avoid it happening in the future. There are three common root causes: physical, human, and organizational.

Physical Causes

Physical causes are any physical objects that prevent the desired outcome from being achieved. An example of a physical cause is that your car gets a flat tire, so you cannot get to work.

Human Causes

Human causes are when a person or persons commit an error that results in a problem. However, human errors are often associated with physical causes. An example would be that your tires were old and needed replacement. Because of this, your tire went flat.

Organizational Causes

Organizational causes occur when the processes or systems of an organization break down. An example is that you brought your car in for an inspection. The technician failed to check your tires because his revised checklist forgot to include this item.

Steps to Doing a Root Cause Analysis

Having discussed the three causes of a problem, you can now proceed with a root cause analysis. The steps are as follows:

Define the Problem

This was discussed in Chapter 2. Using what you know, you need to be able to state the problem clearly.

Collect Data

Gather as much information as you can regarding the problem. Do a thorough investigation of it.

Identify the Potential Causes

When you have collected your data, the next step is to examine any potential causes of the problem. Consider physical, human, and organizational. These are potential causal factors.

Determine the Cause

Look at each causal factor and determine its root cause. To do this, use root cause analysis tools, one of which is the 5 Whys technique that was previously discussed.

Arrive at Solutions

When you have identified the root causes, develop a plan to address them and implement them.

Another part of the problem-solving process is decision-making. This is the topic of the next chapter.

CHAPTER 4

Strategic Decision-Making Strategies

Strategic decision-making is the process of choosing the best option for achieving your desired outcome. There is no one-size-fits-all strategy for making decisions. Instead, there are various models for making decisions. Each of these models has its benefits and limitations. We will now explore some of these decision-making models:

Structured Decision-Making

The structured decision-making process is an ideal model to use for dealing with personal problems. **It can be applied to a variety of situations, including:**

- Conflict

- Coping with loss

- Work challenges

- Difficulties in parenting

Such situations often lead to feelings of stress. By going through the various steps of the structured problem-solving strategy, you can reduce your stress by clarifying the problem and finding potential resolutions. **The following are the steps:**

Step 1: Clarifying the Situation

At this stage, you want to identify the symptoms you are experiencing due to the issue. Symptoms may include things like anxiety, stress, or depression. When you identify what you are feeling, identify the problems you are experiencing now.

Step 2: Define the Problems

Take time to reflect on the problems that you identified in Step 1. As you learned earlier in this book, define each of your problems. Make them specific and clearly stated. You want to have a clear understanding of what is bothering you.

Step 3: Generate Solutions

For each problem that you identified in Step 1, brainstorm potential solutions. Make a list of as many possible solutions as you can. Do not be concerned with their viability at this stage.

Step 4: Evaluate the Solutions

At this step, evaluate each solution on your list regarding its viability. Also, determine what the pros and cons are for each solution.

Step 5: Select the Optimal Solution

Determine which solutions on your list are most optimal for you. Which solutions are most likely to get the results that you are looking for? **When you have identified your top solutions, ask yourself the following questions for each one:**

1. What do I believe would be the best outcome if I implemented this solution?

2. What would be the worst possible outcome if I implemented this solution?

3. All things considered, what would most likely be the outcome if I implanted this solution?

Based on your answers to these questions, select the solution that you believe would achieve your best outcome.

Step 6: Create a Plan of Action

Having selected your solutions, create an action plan for their implementation. Ask yourself what the first step would be to get things going, what would be the next step, and so on until you have identified all the steps you would need to implement your plan.

Besides outlining your steps, ask yourself the following questions:

1. Whose help would I need to make my plan successful?

2. How much time should I allow for each step to be completed? Do I need to get the problem resolved by a certain date?

3. What obstacles do I expect to encounter as I execute my plan? How will I manage them?

4. Do I need to rehearse any difficult parts of the plan, such as role-playing a difficult conversation?

5. When will I check in on my progress with my plan? How often do I need to check in?

In addition to asking yourself these questions, identify your resources for facing obstacles. Your resources may be:

- Your personal strengths, talents, and skills.

- Your stress relief strategies and ways that you can relax.

- Your social support and connections.

- Self-help resources, such as books and videos.

Step 7: Take Action

You know the result you want, and you have developed a detailed plan. It is time to act!

Step 8: Evaluate

Review how you are progressing with your plan. Ask yourself the following:

1. Am I moving closer to achieving my outcome?

2. Do I see any changes in my situation due to following my plan?

3. Do I need to make any adjustments to my plan?

If your plan is working, keep going with it. If you notice that your plan needs fine-tuning, make the needed adjustments. If you see no improvement, develop a new plan. Remember, you might not solve your problem on your first try. That's okay. Problem solving is a learning experience. It may be that your problem is bigger than you thought. Revise your plan and try again. **Ask yourself the following questions:**

- In what areas did my plan work?

- In what areas did my plan not work?

- Given how my plan worked out, what did I learn about my situation? How did it change things?

- What can I do differently next time?

Rational Decision Model

The rational decision-making model uses a logical and systematic approach to decision-making. Its steps include:

1. Defining the problem

2. Developing and evaluating potential solutions

3. Implementing them

4. Evaluating their success

The benefits of the rational model are that it is objective, consistent, and transparent. It allows you to avoid biases or errors that may influence your decision-making. However, this model has its drawbacks. It assumes you have all the necessary information to make the best decision. In reality, we can never get all the information we need to make the best decision, as unknowns are always involved. I may gather a lot of information for planning my next vacation. However, there will be many unknowns, such as the weather and traffic conditions. Also, gathering data can be time-consuming. This model also ignores human factors such as emotions, values, intuition, and creativity.

The Intuitive Decision-Making Model

Unlike the rational decision-making model, which is based on information, the intuitive decision-making model is based on your instincts, gut feelings, and experience. Because of this, it is useful when you must make quick decisions.

It also allows for more creativity and flexibility when making decisions. Further, the intuitive decision-making technique offers the benefit of being more adaptable when confronted with complex or uncertain situations with a lack of information.

The limitations of this model are that it can be inconsistent, subjective, and vulnerable to personal biases. Further, it may overlook important information that could affect your decision-making. The intuitive model normally addresses daily operations where an immediate decision is needed.

Rational or Intuitive: Which Should You Choose?

When determining which model to use, it is best to think about the specific situation you are dealing with. When deciding which model to use, consider the nature of the problem, the availability of quality information, and the decision-makers' preferences.

Many use the rational model to analyze the situation and the intuitive model to make the final decision. Either way, it is best to learn how to balance both models during decision-making.

SWOT Analysis

SWOT is the acronym for the areas of analysis this method offers. **These areas include your:**

S: Strengths

W: Weaknesses

O: Opportunities

T: Threats

Strengths include things like:

- An informed and motivated sales staff

- Positive customer relationships

- Strong internal communication

- Effective marketing strategies

Weakness includes things like:

- Cash flow issues

- Ineffective recordkeeping

- Out-of-date marketing data

- Issues with meeting deadlines

Opportunities include things like:

- A loyal customer base

- Your competition's product is more expensive or of lower quality

- Customer demand

- Your product can reach the market at key times, such as before Christmas

Threats include things like:

- Your competitors' products

- Your competitor's new advertising campaign

- A competitor has opened a shop near you

- Economic downturn

SWOT analysis is used primarily for making business decisions. It can identify the strengths, weaknesses, opportunities, and threats of a project or your competition. **SWOT analysis can be used in situations such as:**

- Determining the benefits of new business opportunities

- Responding to emerging trends

- Implementing the latest technologies

- Responding to changes to your competition's operations

How to Use SWOT Analysis

When using the SWOT analysis, you look at external and internal factors that may affect your business. Internal factors include your business's strengths and weaknesses, while external factors include your opportunities and threats. More specifically, external factors are those that are independent of your business, such as technology or the marketplace.

The following are the steps for using SWOT analysis:

1. Determine Your Objective or Define the Problem

Review Chapter 2 for details.

2. Do Your Research

Research what is happening with your business and your industry. Also, do market research.

3. Identify Your Business's Strengths

Make a list of your business's strengths. You do not need to worry about prioritizing them at this step of the process.

4. Identify your Business's Weaknesses

Make a list of your business's weaknesses. Your list can prove to be an important resource not just now but also in the future. Looking back, you can use your list to determine how much your business has grown.

5. Identify Your Business Opportunities

Do not confuse your external opportunities with your strengths. Remember, your business opportunities would still exist even if you were not in business.

6. Identify Your Potential Threats

Make a list of the potential threats to your business. Remember, an external threat would still exist even if your business did not exist. An example of this would be high interest rates or increased competition.

7. Create Your Priorities

After completing the previous steps, you will end up with four lists. Place these lists side by side to get an overall picture of what is happening with your business. For each list, prioritize the items according to what is most important to you. You can then work on those items. When those items have been resolved, you can address the next item on the list.

8. Create a Strategy to Deal With Your SWOT Issues

Use your prioritized lists to answer the following questions:

1. How could we utilize our strengths to take advantage of our opportunities?

2. How could we utilize our strengths to address the identified threats?

3. What must happen to overcome our weaknesses and take advantage of the identified opportunities?

4. What must happen for us to overcome our weaknesses so that we can better deal with the identified potential threats?

Upon answering these questions, you can utilize your SWOT analysis to create strategies for accomplishing your business goals.

The Advantages and Limitations of the SWOT Analysis

The advantage of using the SWOT analysis is that anyone with business knowledge can effectively use it. It is also good to use when you have limited time to plan.

The limitations of the SWOT analysis are:

- You cannot prioritize your defined problems.

- It will not provide you with a clear solution to your business problems.

- While it will provide much information, not all will be relevant.

Whenever we are making decisions, it is important that we are aware of any biases we may have. Such biases can prevent us from clearly understanding the nature of the problem and finding a solution. We will discuss this in the next section.

Heuristics and Decision-Making

The daily decisions we make may be in the hundreds or even the thousands. Many decisions can be so mundane that we may not even be aware that we are making them. **For example:**

- "What do I want to wear today?"

- "What do I want to watch on television?"

- "What do I want for dinner?"

Our lives would come to a standstill if we had to think through every decision that we had to make. Thankfully, our brains have a way to help us make decisions quickly by taking shortcuts. These shortcuts are known as heuristics. Heuristics allow us to quickly think through our options and reach a decision about our problem. **Here is an example:**

Let's say you are about to drive to work when you suddenly remember that you need to pick up some things from the grocery store. However, the grocery store is out of your way. You realize that going to the grocery store will make you late for work, so you decide to go there on your way home at the end of the day. Your ability to quickly make that decision is an example of a heuristic.

While heuristics have their advantages, they also have disadvantages, which are cognitive biases. Cognitive biases are irrational tendencies in our thinking due to limitations in our ability to process information. We all have cognitive biases. If we are aware of them, we can help prevent them from influencing our decision-making.

Heuristic Types

There are many types of heuristics that lead to cognitive bias. The following are some of the more common ones:

Availability

The availability heuristic causes us to make decisions based on how easily we can retrieve information from our memories. Because we easily access these memories, we believe that their occurrence is more common than they are. Here is an example:

Let's say you have the thought you could fly to an event being held out of state. You suddenly remember recent news stories about plane crashes. As a result, you decide to drive to the event instead.

The fact is that car crashes are far more common than plane crashes. However, because you have memories of these news stories, you believe that plane crashes are more common than they actually are.

Familiarity

We are influenced by the familiarity heuristic by having a more favorable opinion of the things we are familiar with than novel things. This would apply to people and places as well.

We tend to favor people and places we know over those we are unfamiliar with. This favoritism occurs even when a new option would be more beneficial to us. An example is that we may favor the fast food we are used to eating over trying a vegan meal for the first time.

Representativeness

The representativeness heuristic causes us to make decisions based on comparisons of the present moment to our most representative mental concepts. Example: A man walks by you with a stern look on his face. He reminds you of your father, who was strict. You assume that this man is also strict. This is a heuristic bias because you cannot tell if this man is strict just by the expression on his face.

Affect

When we make decisions while being influenced by our emotions, we are experiencing the affect heuristic. An example of this was research where it was found that people tend to focus on the benefits of a decision when they are in a positive mood, while focusing on the downsides of a decision when they are in a negative mood (Cherry, 2023).

Anchoring

With the anchoring heuristic, we are overly influenced by the original information we receive. When this occurs, it makes it more difficult to consider other options. An example of this can be found in our purchasing behavior. We go with the first offer, thinking that it is a great deal without doing any comparative shopping.

Scarcity

The scarcity heuristic is frequently used in advertising. This heuristic is founded on the principle that the scarcer something is, the more valuable it will be. Advertisements convey this with slogans such as "This offer is available for a limited time only."

How Heuristics Create Bias

Heuristics create errors in our thinking by making it more difficult for us to see alternative solutions or ideas. Additionally, heuristics can lead to the formation of prejudices and stereotypes. This is because these mental shortcuts cause us to place people into categories while overlooking relevant information.

How to Deal with Heuristics

As mentioned earlier, all of us are influenced by heuristics. They are just an aspect of how our brains work. You cannot eliminate heuristics, but you can minimize their impact on you. The fundamental way of doing so is through self-awareness. The following are ways to help you achieve this:

Avoid Rushed Decision-Making

You are more likely to make an error in your decision-making when making quick decisions or feel pressured to do so. When possible, step away from the situation and distract yourself by doing something else. When you feel ready, return to the decision at hand. Doing this will allow you to develop a fresh perspective or notice things you previously overlooked.

Know Your Outcome

When making a decision, remind yourself of the outcome you want. What is it that you want to achieve? How will your decision affect others? Is this the best decision for everyone involved?

Manage Your Emotions

Making quick decisions can often lead to errors in our decision-making because we are likely to be affected by our emotions. When this happens, it can lead us to make decisions without looking at the big picture.

Beware of All-or-Nothing Thinking

All-or-nothing thinking is a cognitive distortion that we commonly experience. We may blame ourselves for making a minor error or focus on negative feedback while brushing off the positive ones. Our brains tend to lean more toward negative than positive experiences. This negative focus prevents us from challenging our thinking or looking for alternative options.

An example of this is that you are having an employee review. Your supervisor tells you about all the positive things you are doing but then informs you of an area you could improve on. When you have all-or-nothing thinking, you will discard all the positive things said and dwell on the fact that you were told you could improve.

Take time to challenge your thinking and look for different perspectives. You can also do this by talking to others whom you respect. Doing so may lead you to other options you may not have considered.

CHAPTER 5

Creative Problem-Solving Techniques

We have covered a lot of information about problem solving in this book. Now that you know this subject, it is time to look at blending creativity with problem solving. Creative problem solving offers you greater flexibility to explore solutions. **We will now look at different methods:**

Creative Problem Solving

Creative problem solving (CPS) is often used in organizational settings, but you can apply the basic principles to your personal life. The idea behind CPS is to be creative in your approach to finding solutions to problems.

The following are the basic steps to creative problem solving:

1. **Gain Clarity**

For this step, you need to clarify your goal or the nature of the problem you are trying to solve. You can do this by asking yourself clarifying questions and getting as much information as possible about the situation.

As for questioning, you need to find the fundamentals of your goal or problem. **The following are examples of such questions:**

Questions for Goals:

My goal is to take a European vacation next summer.

Question 1: Why do I want to take a European vacation?

Answer: Because I always wanted to see Europe. Also, I need a vacation.

Question 2: Why have I always wanted to see Europe?

Answer: Because I heard it is a lot different to where I live.

Question 3: Why do I need a vacation?

Answer: Because I have been working very hard the last few months.

My fundamental goal is to see something different and take time off from work. Knowing this, I can take a European vacation or find other options that meet my needs. The advantage is that I may save a lot of money if I can meet these needs by going elsewhere.

Questions for Problems

My problem: I want to be in a relationship but cannot find someone.

Question 1: Why can't I find someone?

Answer: Because I have a hard time meeting people.

Question 2: Why do I have a hard time meeting people?

Answer: Because I feel awkward around others.

Question 3: Why do I feel awkward around other people?

Answer: Because I do not feel confident.

My fundamental problem is that I do not have confidence. I need to address this problem before I try a relationship.

By gaining clarity on your goals and problems, you are more likely to be successful in getting what you want.

2. Brainstorm

Once you gain clarity about the problem, the next step is to brainstorm ideas for ways to solve it. When brainstorming, you need to write down every idea that comes to mind, even if it seems unrealistic. The idea is not to put up any roadblocks in your mind. You want your thoughts to flow.

3. Evaluate and Develop

After you brainstorm ideas, the next step is to evaluate your ideas and develop the best one. To do this, go through each idea on your brainstorming list and evaluate it by asking yourself the **following questions:**

1. Does this idea bring me closer to achieving my goal or resolving my problem? If so, keep it on your list. If not, cross it off.

2. Is the idea realistic and practical? If so, keep it on your list. If not, cross it off.

Next, look at the remaining ideas on your list and choose the one you feel is the best. When you select an idea, develop it.

Example:

My goal: Take a vacation where I could see something different.

The best idea on my brainstorming list was:

"Hike the Grand Canyon."

This idea needs to be developed so that it is more specific. To develop this idea into a goal, I rephrased it as:

"I will schedule a vacation to the Grand Canyon within six months from today."

In developing this idea, I know what I am going to do and when I will be doing it.

My problem: I do not have confidence.

The best idea on my brainstorming list was:

"I will talk to a counselor."

This idea needs to be developed so that it is more specific. To develop this idea into a goal, I rephrased it as:

"I will schedule an appointment with a counselor within one week to discuss my lack of confidence."

In developing this idea, I know what I am going to do and when I will be doing it.

4. Take Action

Now that you have developed your idea, the next step is implementing it. It is time to act!

5. Revaluate

As you act on your idea, pay attention to the feedback that you receive. In other words, is the action you are taking bringing you closer to your goal or solving your problem? If so, continue with your plan. If not, adjust your plan until you get the results you are looking for.

The next model for creative problem solving is the SCAMPER method.

The SCAMPER Method

The SCAMPER method is an effective way to generate creative thinking. For many, coming up with creative thoughts can be challenging. SCAMPER generates creativity by looking at what is happening currently and making modifications to create something new. **SCAMPER is an acronym for:**

S: Substitute

C: Combine

A: Adapt

M: Modify

P: Put to another use

E: Eliminate

R: Reverse

Substitute

Substitute refers to thinking about what could be replaced, be it people, rules, materials, processes, or products.

Example: The innovation of food items, such as substituting the traditional ingredients of the burrito and creating the sushi burrito.

Combine

Combine refers to the combining of features or components. It's about synthesizing product features or combining different teams to work on a project.

Example: The creation of the smartphone combined the features of different devices for listening to music, accessing the internet, taking pictures, and placing phone calls.

Adapt

Adapt refers to making minor tweaks to improve a product or process. It could also mean taking the solution to one problem and adapting it to address a different problem. It can also apply to making changes to a process or product to better adapt to lifestyle changes.

Example: Netflix began as a DVD rental service but adapted itself by becoming a streaming service.

Modify

Modify refers to making modifications to change outcomes. It could be modifying a process to change outcomes or efficiency. It can also mean modifying a product's appearance or size.

Example: Companies may modify their logo to change how they are perceived by the public.

Put To Another Use

Put to another use refers to changing how a product or service is utilized. Could your product be used in a different field or industry? Could your product be used differently from the way it was initially intended?

Example: The "Put to another use" principle is becoming widely used to address environmental concerns. For instance, Adidas has begun to make shoes that are made out of recycled ocean waste (The Decision Lab, n.d.).

Eliminate

Eliminate refers to removing certain aspects of a product to simplify or streamline it.

Example: The invention of Bluetooth earphones eliminated the wiring of traditional earphones, and Apple eliminated the CD drive of their laptop computers to make them lighter and thinner.

Reverse

Reverse refers to changing the sequence of how business is done. With this principle, you would ask yourself, "What could be rearranged?" or "What could be swapped or flipped?"

The reverse principle is particularly effective for changing one's decision-making approach.

Example: Let's say that a company has traditionally used the top-down approach to decision-making, meaning that it focuses on the big picture rather than the micro level. It may benefit from the bottom-up approach, where the focus is on specific characteristics. Doing this may provide insights that were missed under the traditional approach.

In the next chapter, we will look at problem solving in higher domains.

CHAPTER 6

Advanced Levels of Problem Solving

There are situations when problem solving involves issues that can affect an entire company, country, or even the world. We will briefly examine problem solving as it relates to business leadership, technology, and complex problems.

Business Leadership

In most situations, business leaders depend on their employees to help them solve organizational problems. To do so, leaders need the following skills:

Framing of the Problem

Framing the problem is the same thing as defining the problem, which was discussed earlier. This step is critical as there is no one correct way to frame the problem. However, the way you frame the problem will determine the course of action that you take. For this reason, business leaders must have a clear understanding of the problem. **Here is an example:**

Let's say that you run a company that produces frozen dinners and your sales are plunging.

To frame this problem, you may want to inquire about the following:

- What is the status of the frozen dinner market?

- Do we need to improve the quality of our frozen dinners?

- Is the problem a marketing issue?

- Is it a larger issue that impacts how we produce and market frozen foods?

You need to correctly frame the problem so that it reflects your company's priorities and your employees can generate the right ideas for your company.

Empathy

When solving the problem, it is important to have empathy for all stakeholders who are affected by it. Empathy is the ability to relate to the emotions and experiences of others. This would include:

- How your employees are affected by declining sales

- Your customers, who normally purchase your product

- How your shareholders are affected by the drop in sales

It is important to have empathy because you need it to understand the root of the problem and the perspectives of others. As discussed earlier, heuristics and other forms of cognitive bias can distort our perspectives. It is for this reason that it is important to be empathetic when getting feedback from others.

Overcoming Cognitive Fixedness

Cognitive fixedness is a form of cognitive bias where we view situations through the filters of our past experiences. Leaders need to overcome this so that they can be receptive to potential solutions they may not have otherwise considered. For example, you may believe that making frozen dinners that are all-natural is a prohibited cost. Is there an alternative way that would allow you to do so at a lower price?

Create a Safe Atmosphere

As stated earlier, leaders rely on their people to help solve organizational problems. It is for this reason that a leader must create a safe atmosphere where everyone feels comfortable expressing their ideas and opinions. Only then can a leader get the quality feedback they need to make decisions.

Technology and Problem Solving

There is a strong relationship between technology and organizational problem solving. The problem-solving process involves gathering data, analyzing it, and then making a decision. At the organizational level, technology is a major source of that data. **The following are examples of this:**

Enterprise Resource Planning

Enterprise resource planning (ERP) is software used by organizations to manage daily business activities such as supply chain operations, risk management, procurement, and accounting.

While ERP has been traditionally used by large corporations, software companies have increasingly developed versions for use by small businesses.

Collaboration Tools

Some businesses have multiple locations that operate independently of each other. Collaboration tools allow these branches to maintain consistency with the policies and practices of corporate headquarters. Using video webcasts and conference calls, all locations can ensure that they are working in coordination with each other.

Business Analysis Tools

While larger businesses have departments that specialize in business analytics, the small business owner has traditionally had to conduct all these functions themselves. They have to wear multiple hats, such as for accounting, payroll, procurement, and training. Some small businesses have outsourced these functions; however, an alternative is business analysis tools. Small businesses can use business analysis tools to crunch data so that they can make strategic decisions.

Decision Support System

Decision support systems (DSS) collect raw business data that businesses can use to forecast potential problems. While DSS is not something new, their processing ability has greatly increased over the years. Their ability to help business owners foresee problems is beyond what humans can do alone. DDS is also being used as a form of artificial intelligence by professionals, such as doctors. It allows them to make better decisions when presented with problems involving patient care.

Managing Complex Problems

The COVID-19 pandemic was a problem that impacted everyone. No part of the globe was unaffected. It also meant that the entire globe had to be part of the problem-solving effort. Though we did not have a solution, we knew we had to do something. The COVID-19 pandemic was a perfect example of a complex problem.

Complex problems were previously discussed in Chapter 2. However, we will go into more detail here due to their significance. **The following are some characteristics of complex problems:**

1. There are circumstances when addressing complex problems is imperative, such as the COVID-19 pandemic. If we had done nothing about COVID-19, the impact on the world would have been even worse.

2. Often, complex problems are managed rather than solved. Complex problems are called "complex" for a reason. There are so many variables involved, some of which are unknown.

A simple problem has order to it. There is a cause and an effect. Because of all the variables involved, complex problems are unordered. When dealing with complex problems, the idea is to provide interventions that move the problems from being unordered toward being more ordered, allowing them to be better understood.

With the COVID-19 pandemic, we countered with vaccines, lockdowns, and travel regulations. These measures brought greater order to the problem and made it more manageable.

3. The interventions used to manage simple problems have their own systemic impacts.

The interventions used during the pandemic had their own systematic impact. Examples are economic hardship, working from home, and a greater political divide.

It was mentioned earlier that there are occasions when it is imperative to address complex problems. The COVID-19 pandemic is an example of this. One reason why addressing the pandemic was imperative was because its effects could not be ignored. People were becoming ill and dying. The political will to take action was there because of that.

Now, compare this to another complex problem: climate change. Though climate change is an existential threat, the political will to take it seriously is lacking. Unlike the COVID-19 pandemic, the effects of climate change are not as evident to most people. It is a more abstract threat.

Conclusion

Problems are an inevitable part of life. As long as we are alive, we will experience them. Most people have a negative attitude toward problems. However, you can reverse that attitude and appreciate your problems. Problems challenge us to learn and grow as people. By using problem-solving techniques, you can reap the benefits of each problem that comes your way.

By improving your problem-solving skills, you will become more effective at resolving future problems and achieving your goals. More importantly, you will further enhance your inner world. You will feel more confident and happier because you will know that you can handle future problems. Further, you will be a more attractive job candidate as managers are looking for people who can problem solve.

This guide is not a one-time read. Instead, treat it as a user's manual. Refer back to it whenever you need to make an important decision. It takes time and practice to develop problem-solving skills.

Book 3

A Better Choice

A Guide to Logical Reasoning

How to Use Logical Reasoning to Improve Your Life

Introduction

We live in a time where we are bombarded by information, largely due to the internet. We are also experiencing a deepening of the polarization of America, where extreme political views are gaining acceptance. For many of us, economic times are becoming increasingly difficult due to rising house, gas, and food prices. These forces make logical decision-making as important as ever.

Our decisions can shape our lives for the better or worse. Who should you vote for? Which brand should you purchase? How can you make yourself more promotable at your job? What can you do to increase your income? How can you improve your grades at school? The answer to all these questions lies in the decisions that you make. The quality of our decisions determines the quality of our lives. To make the best decisions, we must use logical reasoning.

Logical reasoning involves using rationale to come to a conclusion about a given statement or to solve a problem. Using logical reasoning, you can make decisions based on reason rather than fear or the opinions of others who may be trying to persuade you but do not have your best interests in mind.

In this book, you will learn about the different kinds of logical reasoning, how to develop the skills for logical reasoning, and how to apply them in your daily life. This book is intended for everyone to read, as we must make important life decisions. It is for the student who wants to prepare for standardized tests. It is for the employee who wants to get ahead in their career. It is for the voter who wants to break through the political noise and choose the best candidate. Regardless of where you are in your life, this book will show you how to make quality decisions for your life and those you love.

The following are just some of the things that you will learn in this book:

- The basic principles of logical reasoning

- How to avoid falling for commonly used logical fallacies

- How to develop critical thinking skills

- How to apply logical reasoning in your daily life

- Exercises and activities to practice logical reasoning skills

Get ready for a transformative journey where you can change your thinking and become a better version of yourself!

CHAPTER 1

Foundations of Logical Reasoning

As indicated earlier, logical reasoning is a way of thinking where you form a conclusion based on a set of information or premises. When you use logical reasoning, you are being objective and logical in your reasoning. **The following is an example:**

Let's say that someone runs a grocery store and wants to determine whether they are selling more bananas or apples. **To find the answer to the question, they gather the following information:**

1. The number of bananas and apples that were received in the last shipment

2. The amount of bananas and apples that were lost due to damage or spoilage

3. The number of bananas and apples that were sold

Based on this information, the grocer can determine which of the fruits they are selling more of.

If the grocer sold fifty-eight bananas and seventy-five apples during the same period, and there was no loss due to damage or spoilage, they can logically conclude that they sold more apples than bananas.

Again, logical reasoning follows a systematic approach to problem-solving or determining the truth of a statement. The previous example of the grocer is the approach you can use to solve a problem. You are simply gathering information about the problem so that you can solve it.

Other times, someone may make a logical argument. Logical arguments are statements that others may make to explain why they believe something is true. **Examples of this**

include:

- "I never miss a day running except when it rains."

- "Practice leads to mastery. If I practice martial arts, I will become a black belt."

- "I am not feeling well. It must be the leftovers that I ate last night."

The following are steps that you can use to determine the truthfulness of a statement or argument:

- Break the argument down into its components.

- Determine the method of reasoning used.

- Determine if the conclusion makes sense.

Break the Argument Down into Its Components

The first step to determining the truthfulness of an argument is to understand its components. You can see if it contains flaws by breaking down the argument into its components. **For example:**

- "I never miss a day running except when it rains."

- "Practice leads to mastery. If I practice martial arts, I will become a black belt."

- "I am not feeling well. It must be the leftovers that I ate last night."

When we hear such statements, we often do not question their truthfulness. But what if you were a lawyer and cross-examining a witness? Lawyers are great at breaking down arguments to challenge their truthfulness. **The following are examples of this:**

Argument: "I never miss a day running except when it rains."

Breaking down the argument: "You say you never miss a day running except when it rains. What about when it snows? Do you enjoy running when it snows?"

Argument: "Practice leads to mastery. If I practice martial arts, I will become a black belt."

Breaking down the argument: "Does everyone who practices martial arts become a black belt?"

Argument: "I am not feeling well. It must be the leftovers that I ate last night."

Breaking down the argument: "Is it possible that something else made you sick other than the pizza?"

Determine the Method of Reasoning Used

When testing the validity of an argument, it can be helpful to understand the method of reasoning that was used. Two of the commonly used methods are causation and conditional reasoning. **The following is an argument that is based on causation:**

"I am not feeling well. It must be the leftovers that I ate last night."

This argument insinuates that leftovers are the cause of not feeling well. The statement "I am not feeling well" is the premise, while "It must be the leftovers that I ate last night" is the conclusion.

The following is an argument that is based on conditional reasoning:

"Practice leads to mastery. If I practice martial arts, I will become a black belt." In this argument, becoming a black belt is conditional on practicing. The challenge is that becoming a black belt may take more than practice.

Determine If the Conclusion Makes Sense

You can challenge the conclusion of the argument "I am not feeling well. It must be the leftovers that I ate last night."

You can put on your lawyer hat and say, "Is it possible that something else made you sick other than the pizza?" If the answer is "Yes," then you have demonstrated there is a flaw in the conclusion. In this argument, the cause is an opinion rather than a fact.

The statement, "Practice leads to mastery. If I practice martial arts, I will become a black belt," concludes that practice will lead to becoming a black belt. You can challenge this conclusion by determining if this statement is always true. "I can practice martial arts as much as I want. However, if I have limited mobility, I cannot master the movements needed to become a black belt." In this argument, other factors are not considered, making it flawed.

These examples demonstrate why learning to use logical reasoning is important. It will help you make important decisions and uncover the truth of others' arguments. Logical reasoning is also valuable when problem-solving, developing new ideas, and setting goals.

The previous example of the grocer illustrates how logical reasoning can be used in problem-solving. As for developing new ideas, logical reasoning provides a foundation for innovation. Because the grocer is selling more apples than bananas, they can come up with new ideas to increase the sales of bananas, which can also be a goal.

Kinds of Logical Reasoning

There are three major kinds of logical reasoning: seductive, inductive, and abductive. Understanding these three types can help you identify the thinking you and others are using.

Deductive Reasoning

When using deductive reasoning, you use premises to arrive at an indisputable conclusion.

The following are examples:

Example 1

Premise 1: Roads are slippery when wet.

Premise 2: It is raining now.

Conclusion: You need to be cautious when driving.

Example 2

Premise 1: State offices are closed on the holidays.

Premise 2: The Department of Economic Security is a state office.

Conclusion: The Department of Economic Security is closed for Christmas.

Example 3

Premise 1: You have reserved a meeting room for 3 p.m.

Premise 2: It is 3 p.m., and the group that currently uses the room is still there.

Conclusion: The current group is running late with their meeting.

What these examples share is that factual conclusions are derived from factual premises.

The Pros and Cons of Deductive Reasoning

While deductive reasoning provides factual conclusions, it does have its limitations. **The following are the pros and cons of deductive reasoning:**

The Pros

Certainty

Deductive reasoning results in conclusions that we can be certain about. This is because the conclusions are based on logic and the relationships between the premises and conclusions. If mammals have fur and are warm-blooded, and dogs have fur and are warm-blooded, we can logically deduce that dogs are mammals.

Easy to Follow

The process of deductive reasoning is easy to follow. It also makes it easy to accept the conclusion. Again, it is not difficult to see the logic behind the statement: mammals have fur and are warm-blooded, and dogs have fur and are warm-blooded. Thus, dogs are mammals.

Validity

Deductive reasoning leads to valid conclusions if the premises are true. If the conclusion is invalid, it is because of problems with the premises. The premise that mammals have fur and are warm-blooded is true. Also true is that dogs have fur and are warm-blooded. For this reason, the conclusion that dogs are mammals must be true.

Generality

Deductive reasoning allows you to make general inferences or statements. For example, if you know that dogs are mammals, wolves and foxes must also be mammals.

Efficiency

Deductive reasoning is a time-saver because you can quickly conclude without conducting research or experiments. For this reason, deductive reasoning is an effective tool for problem-solving in areas such as science and math.

Testability

Others can authenticate deductive reasoning by confirming that the premises are accurate. By following the steps of deductive thinking, others should agree with the conclusion.

The Cons

Limited Subject Areas

Deductive reasoning can only be applied to mathematical and logical subjects like science. It is less effective in more intuitive areas such as art, philosophy, or history.

Rigid Rule Set

Deductive reasoning follows a rigid set of rules or procedures. Because of this, it does not provide room for creative thinking or thinking outside the box.

An Assumption of Complete Knowledge

When someone uses deductive reasoning, it assumes that they have complete knowledge of the subject area and that all relevant information is available to them. Realistically speaking, these conditions are very difficult to meet. For example, the premise that all mammals have hair, are warm-blooded, and bear live young is untrue. There are a few mammals that lay eggs. Because of this, duck-billed platypuses would not be mammals.

The Deductive Reasoning Process

Deductive reasoning can be applied to your daily life by following a simple process:

1. Identify the problem.

2. Get as much information as you can about the problem.

3. Come up with a theory of how to address the problem.

4. Test your theory.

5. If you do not get the results you are looking for, go back to step 3 and try again. If you get the results you are looking for, you have resolved the problem.

Here is an example:

1. The problem is that a person is not bringing in enough money from their business.

2. They research the problem by looking at their costs, marketing practices, and other relevant business areas.

3. They come up with a theory. They believe they are not marketing effectively and must reduce their supply costs.

4. They test their theory by executing it.

5. After executing their theory, their revenue goes up.

Inductive Reasoning

While deductive reasoning involves taking factual premises and reaching an undisputable conclusion, inductive reasoning involves taking factual premises and reaching a generalized conclusion. In other words, the conclusion is based on probability. **Here is an example:**

You have a jar with 30 marbles in it. The marbles are either black or blue in color. You decide to estimate the number of black and blue marbles. To do this, you randomly take 6 marbles. The 6 marbles consist of 4 black marbles and 2 blue ones. **Since there are 30 marbles in the jar, you estimate that there are 20 black marbles and 10 blue marbles in the jar:**

- 6 (the number of marbles from the sample) x 5 = 30

- So, 4 black marbles x 5 = 20

- Also, 2 blue marbles x 5 = 10

You cannot be sure there are 20 black marbles and 10 blue ones, but there is a high probability of this being true based on the sample you took. There are sections in IQ tests that require the use of inductive reasoning.

The Pros and Cons of Inductive Reasoning

The Pros

The advantage of inductive reasoning is that it allows you to arrive at a probability for a certain situation. For example, you may leave your house and see that it is overcast. Dark clouds are blanketing the sky. Through inductive reasoning, you will equate overcast days with rain. Though there are times when it does not rain on overcast days, you have a chance to prepare in case it does.

Another advantage of inductive reasoning is that it offers permission to be wrong. It takes additional information to determine if your inductive reasoning is correct. An example of this is detective work.

Detectives use inductive reasoning when trying to solve a crime. By finding patterns or observations, they can identify a suspect. They can determine whether their suspicions are valid by doing further detective work. In this manner, inductive reasoning directs them to pursue the truth.

Cons

As with deductive reasoning, inductive reasoning does have its limits. By inductive reasoning, you may believe that all roofs leak at some point just because you had a leaky roof. This reasoning makes sense because roofs are more susceptible to leaks as they get older. However, this reasoning will be proved wrong if you come across someone who has never experienced a leaky roof despite having lived in the same home for a very long time.

Using Inductive Reasoning

To use inductive reasoning, let's go back to the example of the overcast day. Inductive reasoning tells us that rain is probable. You can then use that knowledge to prepare for it.

Abductive Reasoning

With abductive reasoning, you consider all the information available to you, even if that information is incomplete. For this reason, you are reaching an informed guess rather than a factual conclusion. The following are examples of this:

Example 1

In the morning, you wake up and go to the kitchen. You discover a dish of partially eaten pancakes on the table. From this observation, you guess your roommate or partner had to rush to work, so they could not finish breakfast.

Example 2

You are at work and see your supervisor and department manager talking in a conference room. You do not know what their discussion is about, but you assume that it is important.

Example 3

You receive a positive review from your client, so you assume they are happy with your services and will be a repeat customer.

Juries are another example of abductive reasoning. They make an educated guess based on the evidence and witness testimonies.

Pros

Using abductive reasoning can lead to the development of innovative and creative conclusions. An example of this is an artist or scientist whose works result from abductive reasoning and intuition.

Cons

Abductive reasoning is not as dependable as deductive or inductive reasoning. The reason for this is that abductive reasoning can lead to erroneous conclusions. An example is a doctor who misdiagnoses a patient, which can lead to erroneous conclusions that can have serious consequences for the patient.

Logical Fallacies

Has someone ever told you something as though it were factual, yet something about their statement did not seem right? Perhaps they came up with some crazy conclusion, or their argument was based on information that would be difficult to validate. Or maybe their conclusion seemed to come from information taken out of context.

Suppose someone tells you about research that was done on motivating employees. This person tells you that in the experiment, employees were shown images of beautiful nature scenes and baby animals during the first few minutes of their shift.

Soon afterward, it was found that sales at the company increased by 10 percent. This person then tells you confidently that viewing images of nature and baby animals increases the motivation of employees. This person's conclusion is an example of a logical fallacy. It is a logical fallacy because it confuses correlation with causation. In other words, it is based on flawed reasoning.

Just because sales increased after viewing pleasant images does not mean that the viewing of pleasant images caused the increase in sales. There could have been other factors that caused the sales increase. For example, perhaps the economy improved, or the company changed its product line. Perhaps the company was more fully staffed during the study.

Others often use logical fallacies as a tool for persuasion. It is used to get us to think in a way that benefits others' agendas. Logical fallacies are behind what is popularly known as "fake news." It is important to question what you are told if something about the argument seems wrong.

There are different kinds of logical fallacies, and the following are examples of the most common types:

Appeals to Authority

People use this logical fallacy to base their argument on an authoritative source, such as an academic or research study. The implication is that since the argument reflects the knowledge of the authoritative source, the person's argument must be true.

The challenge is that even if the authoritative source is correct, the person who uses it may have misunderstood, misquoted, or overlooked relevant caveats, undermining their argument. **Here is an example:**

Argument: "My doctor told me that the drug XX will help me with my medical disorder. Hence, this drug will help me with my disorder."

This fallacious appeal to authority contains many assumptions. To begin with, is the doctor a medical doctor or a PhD in psychology? If the doctor is a medical doctor, does their training make them an expert in this person's disorder? What if the doctor is a dermatologist, and the person's disorder involves a hormone imbalance? Finally, just because a drug has been proven effective in treating a disorder, does that mean that the drug will be effective with all people and in all situations?

For these reasons, it is important not to rely on a single authority or data source.

False Inductions

A false induction is a fallacy that may cause you to believe there is a causal relationship when there is none. In other words, just because an event occurred before another does not mean that the prior event caused the succeeding one. An example of a false induction was already mentioned earlier in this section. Just because employees view pleasant images at the beginning of their shift does not mean that viewing the images was the cause of the increased sales.

The Slippery Slope

Politicians often use this logical fallacy as an excuse for not supporting a policy. It is used as a fear tactic. The slippery slope argument goes like this: "The worst that could happen will happen if you go ahead with the decision." **Here is an example:**

"If we make marijuana legal, then there will be a push to legalize harder drugs like heroin or cocaine." This argument suggests that the legalization of one substance will result in pressure to legalize other drugs. However, there is no evidence to indicate that would happen.

The Bandwagon Fallacy

This logical fallacy operates by causing us to believe in a proposition or idea based on its popularity with others. This is a fallacy as just because something is popular does not mean it is true or the right thing to do.

For example, let's say that a store surveys its customers to get their opinion on whether it should stay open for twenty-four hours. The survey reveals that staying open twenty-four hours has popular support.

In response to the survey, the store manager jumps to develop a staff schedule to cover the twenty-four-hour operating time. The problem with the store taking action is that the survey does not provide adequate information to justify a decision. The survey does not indicate who the people are that support the extended hours. They may think it is a good idea, but would they purchase late at night or early in the morning? If they made purchases, how often would they do so? Additionally, what would be the costs and benefits for the store? Would the costs be worth the benefits?

To avoid falling for the bandwagon fallacy, you must ask more questions and get more information to determine if the conclusion is correct. Additionally, history has shown that just because an idea is popular does not make it the right thing to do. Take, for example, Hitler and Germany.

The False Dichotomy Fallacy

The false dichotomy fallacy argues for a false choice that we are forced to choose between two options. It's the "either-or" argument. An example was how the Bush administration presented the conflict in Iraq. Bush told an American audience, "You are either with us or against us," meaning that if you supported freedom, you needed to support the invasion of Iraq. Based on his argument, you could not support freedom and be against the invasion.

The false dichotomy fallacy is framed to get you to agree with the other person's argument, as the other option will be viewed as bringing about greater negative consequences. In truth, most dichotomy fallacies are devoid of relevant information that would support a third option. Further, the premise the fallacy is made of may be faulty.

For example, a struggling business may tell its employees there must be layoffs or the company will not survive. However, the company's struggles may have nothing to do with the number of its employees. Its struggle may be because its product is no longer in demand. If the company modified its product to make it more relevant, it may be able to continue.

The Straw Man Fallacy

The straw man fallacy is often used in politics to avoid addressing the real issues. It is done by creating a false argument and then attacking it. By misrepresenting an opposing view, you strengthen your position.

An example would be a politician who proposes to increase funding for solar energy and wind power out of concern for global warming. An opposing candidate may misrepresent this position by saying, "My opponent wants to spend money on unproven technology. If he has his way, he will waste your money and create job losses." By arguing that the proposal is an attack on the taxpayer, the opposing candidate weakens the proposal without addressing the threat of global warming.

The No-True Scotsman Fallacy

The no-true Scotsman fallacy is used to ward off criticisms of a generalized argument. The person making the generalized argument uses this fallacy to dismiss any contrary evidence. **The following is an example:**

A conservative politician is debating a liberal politician on the issue of censorship. The conservative politician states that his party does not stand for censorship. The liberal politician points out that a conservative member from the other party had recently called for the burning of a book. The conservative responded by saying that the party member was not a true conservative.

In this scenario, you can see how the conservative politician dismissed evidence that contradicted his argument by changing the definition of it. In other words, the party member was not a real conservative. When using the no-true Scotsman fallacy, any evidence to the contrary will be shot down as not representative of the general argument.

Observational Selection

With observational selection, you present the points that support your argument but disregard the ones that weaken it. In other words, you are only giving part of the story. **The following is an example:**

A marketing agency tells its clients that television advertisements are more effective than radio ads. The clients are told that television ads reach twice the audience compared to radio and that the audience is more likely to remember television ads.

The marketing agency fails to tell its clients that television ads have a lower return on investment than radio ads. In other words, the more costly television ads may reach a larger audience, but that does not necessarily translate to increased sales conversion.

The False Dilemma Fallacy

The false dilemma fallacy misrepresents complex issues by presenting them as two opposing sides. Rather than acknowledging that complex issues cover a spectrum of perspectives, these issues are presented as though there are only two contrasting positions.

The false dilemma fallacy is increasingly used in today's politics, which can lead to compromising being replaced by extremism. An example is that you need to choose between wealth and ethics. The presumption is that wealth leads to unethical behavior. It ignores the fact that there are businesspeople who are responsible and ethical in their business practices.

The Texas Sharpshooter Fallacy

The Texas sharpshooter fallacy is employed by being selective in the data used to give the appearance of cause and effect when there may be only randomness. **The following is an example:**

A study revealed that the top ten countries where wine is consumed have the lowest incidents of depression. Hence, it concluded that wine prevents depression. In this case, there is only a correlation between wine intake and low depression rates. Any other information that would support a different conclusion was not considered.

The Middle Ground Fallacy

The middle ground fallacy proposes that truth can be found between extreme and conflicting perspectives. It is compromising for the sake of compromising. The challenge with this perspective is that it overlooks that both extremes may be true or both may be false. **The following is an example:**

Bob believes revamping the business website is the most effective way to increase revenue. James is against making any changes to the website. They seek a middle ground by changing just a few of the website pages. But what if Bob is correct in his business assessment and James is wrong? In this case, making a small change to the website will be ineffective. Or what if both are wrong? What if their revenue problems have nothing to do with the website? If this is the case, they have done nothing to address the problem.

The Ad Hominem Fallacy

With the ad hominem fallacy, one party will personally attack the other party instead of using reason to address the weakness of the argument. The ad hominem fallacy is often used against groups or institutions. **Here is an example:**

An activist argues that a minimum wage law should be enacted to avoid worker exploitation. His opponent addresses the activist by saying that his ideas are nonsense and that his problem is that he cannot find a good-paying job.

How to Spot a Logical Fallacy

Everything you need to know to identify a logical fallacy was presented earlier in this chapter! **Let's do a quick review:**

Arguments

Remember that an argument has a basic structure, meaning that it consists of two kinds of statements: a premise and a conclusion. The premise provides the evidence for the conclusion, while the conclusion is inferred from the evidence. **For example:**

1. All mammals are warm-blooded (first premise).

2. Dogs are warm-blooded (second premise).

3. Dogs are mammals (conclusion).

The premise(s) must fully support the conclusion in a logical or valid argument. If this is not true, you are dealing with a logical fallacy. **The following are examples:**

1. Dogs have four legs (first premise).

2. Jack has a dog (second premise).

3. Jack's dog must have four legs (conclusion).

This argument is invalid because Jack's dog may have lost a limb. **Here is another invalid argument:**

1. The Republican Party is against gun control (first premise).

2. My state leans toward the Republican Party (second premise).

3. The voters in my state are against gun control (conclusion).

Without further information, this argument needs to be considered invalid. Not all Republican voters are against gun control. **The following are valid arguments:**

1. To be a licensed psychologist, you must have a master's degree or higher (first premise).

2. James is a licensed psychologist (second premise).

3. James has a master's degree or higher (conclusion).

This argument is valid because the premises fully support the conclusion, as James is a licensed psychologist. **Here is another example:**

1. All mammals are warm-blooded and have hair (first premise).

2. Dogs are warm-blooded and have hair (second premise).

3. Dogs are mammals (conclusion).

Again, both premises support the conclusion that dogs are mammals, as dogs have warm blood and fur.

CHAPTER 2

Developing Critical Thinking

Many people do not utilize critical thinking skills when dealing with important decisions. Fortunately, critical thinking is a soft skill that anyone can develop. The following are some of the aspects of critical thinking:

Analytical Thinking

Analytical and critical thinking are often viewed as being the same thing. Both skills are useful for evaluating information when looking for a solution to a problem. However, they do have their differences. Understanding these differences can help you decide which skills to develop further, which is particularly important when considering a future career.

Critical thinking is a form of analysis that utilizes reasoning to arrive at a conclusion (Wilensky, n.d.). In other words, it is useful for interpreting information for the purpose of decision-making. For example, a mechanic may identify a problem with a car and use critical thinking to determine which tools will be needed to fix the problem.

With analytical thinking, you are analyzing a problem to find a solution (Kaplan, 2023). To do this, you are processing complex information by breaking it down. When using analytical thinking, you are looking for a cause-and-effect relationship between two factors to establish a connection. You are trying to understand the relationship between the two. An example is trying to understand why a certain plant grows better in drier soil.

Both analytical and critical thinking are used to evaluate information, but they do it differently. Analytical thinking uses facts to support evidence, while critical thinking uses facts to make a decision or form an opinion (Indeed, 2023).

Another difference between these two kinds of thinking is the components that they use to reach a conclusion. When using analytical thinking, you focus on evaluating opinions and assumptions, while critical thinking tends to avoid these in favor of accessing data (Indeed, 2023). For these reasons, those who use analytical thinking apply their own reasoning and logic to the situation.

To illustrate the difference between critical and analytical thinking, here are examples from the workplace:

Examples of critical thinking in the workplace include a school principal who uses critical thinking when managing a school's daily operations or a physician who studies a patient's history and current condition to make a diagnosis.

Examples of analytical thinking include an economist who uses analytical thinking to make economic forecasts or a software engineer when making decisions involving creating and implementing new programs.

Evaluating the Evidence

Whether you are using critical or analytical thinking, it is important that you evaluate the evidence. How reliable is the evidence that you have? There is a systematic approach for determining this (Linkedin, 2023). **The following are steps that you can use to determine this:**

1. Identify the Source

When considering information, ask yourself questions such as:

- What is the source of the evidence?

- Is the source credible?

- Do they have authority?

- What are their qualifications?

- Do they have a background relevant to the information they are presenting?

- What is their motivation for presenting the information?

- Do they have an agenda?

- Do they seem impartial or biased?

- Do they have an affiliation with an interest group or organization?

Answering questions like these can help determine how reliable the information is.

Some of the most reliable information can be found in peer-reviewed journals or other scholarly resources. When a material is peer-reviewed, one or more experts with expertise in the field will review the information for accuracy.

2. Review the Methodology

Methodology has to do with how the information was gathered and processed. In other words, how was the information collected? How was it analyzed? How was the information interpreted? Let's say that someone is researching the average person's lifestyle habits. To gather their data, they go to a phone directory and randomly select the names of individuals from the white pages directory. They then call these individuals between 8 a.m. and 5 p.m. From this brief description of the methodology, can you identify its problems?

First, the white pages directory is rarely used anymore due to our current technology. Given this, the phone numbers listed in the white pages will most likely be for landline phones. Who uses a landline phone anymore? Secondly, most people are at work between 8 a.m. and 5 p.m. So, most people who would be home during these hours are probably not working. So, how is it that the information that is collected from this study reflects the average person?

3. Context and Relevance

At this step, you would compare the context and relevancy of the evidence to the situation you are dealing with. **You want to ask questions like:**

- How relevant is this information to the problem I am trying to solve?

- How does this information compare with the existing knowledge in this area?

- If the source provides an alternative view of the situation that differs from other sources, how does it explain that difference?

Asking these kinds of questions will help determine the relevancy of the evidence.

4. What is the Impact of the Evidence?

This fourth step involves determining how impactful the evidence is. **Ask yourself questions like:**

- How does the evidence challenge or support the issue being faced?

- How does the evidence affect your understanding or opinion of the situation?

- Will the evidence affect your decision-making or behavior?

- Does this evidence contribute to innovation or improvement in your field of study?

An example of this step would be in health care. When developing new drugs, they are checked for both statistical and clinical significance. While a new drug may be statistically significant, it may not be clinically significant. The drug must offer meaningful improvement for the patient to be clinically significant.

Let's say the drug is tested, and it is found to reduce patients' pain levels by a few points (on a scale from 1 to 10, it drops from 7 to 6.5). Though this may be statistically significant, it is not clinically significant, as the patient has shown no meaningful improvement.

Asking questions like those previously mentioned will help determine if the evidence is significant to your situation.

5. Apply the Standards of Critical Thinking

In this final step, you can evaluate the evidence by utilizing the standards and criteria for critical thinking. **Ask yourself:**

- What standards and criteria am I using to evaluate the relevance and quality of the evidence?

- What are the strengths and weaknesses of the evidence?

- How do I justify my evaluation of the evidence?

By asking these questions, you will know whether you're basing your determination on critical thinking, emotions, biases, or intuition.

Problem-Solving Strategies

There are a variety of strategies for solving problems, each one suited for a different kind of problem. You should experiment with these strategies until you find your best one. **The following are some of the more common ones:**

Do What Worked for You Before

This may sound obvious, but think about how you dealt with a similar problem. If what you did worked for you, try using it in the current situation.

Brainstorming

Brainstorming is an effective way to come up with solutions. When brainstorming, you come up with as many ideas as possible, no matter how crazy they seem. The idea is to get into a flow of consciousness. You can check for the viability of the ideas when you finish brainstorming. Brainstorming is even more effective as a team, giving you different perspectives.

Work Backward

Working backward is another name for reverse engineering. In your mind, imagine that your problem has already been solved. Use this as a starting point and then work backward. Retrace the steps you would take until you get to where you are now. Doing this will help you identify which actions are most effective.

The Kipling Method

This strategy involves asking yourself the following questions:

- What is the problem?

- What makes this problem important?

- When did the problem occur? When does it need to be taken care of?

- What caused the problem to occur?

- Where is the problem located?

- Who is affected by the problem?

By answering these questions, you may find potential solutions.

Make a Diagram of It

Some problems are difficult to solve by just thinking about them as they may be complex and have different moving parts. For such problems, try drawing a diagram to capture the details of the problem. By doing this, you may see what areas need improvement.

Trial and Error

Try the trial and error approach when you have identified several potential solutions to a problem. By doing this, you can discover which solution is the most effective.

Get Your Sleep

Determining the best solution to a problem requires going through a process. This is the reason you need to get the proper amount of rest. Getting a good night's sleep can bring you clarity and improve your perspective on the situation.

Talk to Others

Ask others for their opinions regarding your situation. By talking to others, you can get different perspectives you may not have considered. It is important to realize that others may have the knowledge, skills, or experience you do not.

Use the Pareto Principle

Also known as the 80/20 rule, the Pareto principle states that only 20 percent of what we do accounts for 80 percent of our results (MindTools, n.d.). For example, 20 percent of a company's sales reps make 80 percent of the total sales. You can use the Pareto principle to narrow down where you look for the cause of the problem. Additionally, it can be used to narrow down where you look for the solution.

The Problem-Solving Process

In the previous section, you learned about different strategies for problem-solving. Whatever strategy you choose, there is a systematic process that you can use to solve the problem. It is important to note that this process is intended for complex problems an organization may experience. However, you can modify the process to address personal problems. **The following is the five-step process for finding possible solutions:**

1. Identify the Problem

This first step involves identifying the problem that you are trying to solve. More specifically, you want to identify the root cause of the problem. This is the step where you gather as much information as possible, keeping in mind the quality of the information (see the previous section, *Evaluating the Evidence*).

2. Break It Down

When the problem has been identified, the next step is to break it down into steps that you can take to address it. When the steps have been identified, you can set time frames for when they need to be accomplished.

3. Come Up with Potential Solutions

For this step, you want to brainstorm possible solutions for the steps you identified in the previous section. When doing this step, it is important to remember that you are not evaluating solutions. Instead, you are coming up with potential solutions.

4. Evaluate the Solutions

In this step, you can narrow down the potential solutions that you came up with in the previous step. **When narrowing down the solutions, consider the following:**

- Will others who are affected by the problem agree to the solution?

- Does the solution support the goal that you are trying to achieve?

- Is the solution likely to yield the desired outcomes?

- Can the solution be realistically executed, given the current restraints and resources?

- Will the solution resolve the problem without creating unintended consequences?

5. Carry Out the Solution and Monitor

When you have identified and evaluated the solution, it is time to execute it and act on it. At the same time, you need to monitor the solution to confirm that it is working. If the solution is not working, repeat these steps again.

A Problem-Solving Example

6. Having problem-solving skills is foundational to making good decisions. **The following is an example of a problem-solving process used by a business:**

Company A is a SaaS (software as a service) brand experiencing declining customer rates or churn rates (customers leaving the business). Company A first needs to identify the problem, which is its churn rates.

Having identified the problem, it must next find out the root cause of the problem. The root cause of the company's problem could be anything from its email marketing campaigns to the customer service experience. If more than one problem was identified, each problem would need its own problem-solving process.

If the issue is with email marketing, problem-solving strategies can be used to find a solution. Perhaps the solution is to find ways to excite customers by offering added value while supplementing that with bonuses, discounts, or special offers. Doing this may encourage customers to maintain their monthly subscriptions.

Another potential solution is offering added incentives, such as premium services, at no extra charge when customers maintain yearly subscriptions.

Whatever solutions the company agrees upon, it establishes time frames to achieve them. Then, managers can monitor the progress of each solution and identify the ones that yield the most effective results.

CHAPTER 3

Practical Applications of Logical Reasoning

In this book, we have covered a lot of information about logical reasoning. Whether you are aware of it or not, you most likely encounter numerous situations during your day where logical reasoning can be used to achieve better outcomes for yourself. This chapter will explore how this information can be applied every day.

Logical Reasoning in Daily Life

There are too many situations in your daily life where logical reasoning can be called upon. For this reason, we will focus on two all-encompassing areas: decision-making and communication.

Decision-Making

As we go about our daily lives, we encounter countless situations that require us to make decisions. When we discuss decision-making, we also include problem-solving as part of deciding the best solution. **Logical reasoning allows us to:**

- Identify the root cause of situations.

- Evaluate potential solutions.

- Decide on the best course of action to take.

Logical reasoning allows us to make decisions driven by critical thinking rather than our emotions or biases. The result is greater success in our personal and professional lives. An important aspect of making good decisions is obtaining quality information. **The following is an example:**

Fred has his eye on a pricey car that he wants to purchase. He starts to gather information about the car, such as its features, value, and mileage. After doing his research, Fred remains uncertain. He talks to a friend with the same car to gain further information and asks about his experience. By getting reliable information, Fred can make the best decision for himself.

Effective Communication

Today's world is bombarded with information due to twenty-four-hour news cycles, the internet, and social media. Logical reasoning skills are essential for determining which information offers value and which is just noise. Logical reasoning does this by getting you to analyze the reasoning and arguments out there.

In developing logical reasoning skills, you learn to organize your thoughts and make rational connections between them. The ability to do this leads to being able to communicate logically. You can present your ideas concisely and clearly, making them easily understood by others.

Other benefits of communicating logically include being more persuasive and effective in conflict resolution. It is easier to gain acceptance of your ideas if you can logically express yourself. Similarly, finding common ground and mutually agreeable solutions is easier when you can communicate logically. **The following are suggestions for communicating logically:**

- Be clear and concise in your communication.

- Avoid using technical terms or jargon.

- When making claims, provide evidence, including personal experiences, statistics, or expert opinions.

- Be open to other perspectives if others disagree with you.

The following are scenarios for logical communication:

- You are asking your manager for a raise. The way to do this logically is to point out to your manager how you consistently exceeded sales quotas, took on extra projects, or received feedback.

- If you are in a relationship and are arguing over house chores, you can use logic to resolve the conflict by pointing out that you both have full-time jobs and are both responsible for house chores.

- If you are learning about a new concept, you can use logic to help understand it. To do this, break down the concept into smaller parts. For each part, identify the key principles. You can then look for real-life examples of how the concept appears. **Here is an example:**

If the concept of symbiosis is being learned, break down the concept. In symbiosis, two organisms coexist with each other. Further, each organism benefits from the other. An example of a situation where two organisms coexist with each other is marriage.

Logical Reasoning in Professional Settings

Developing logical reasoning skills can significantly affect your career or business success. Knowing how to solve problems can make you valuable to your employer. Knowing the decision-making process will determine your business success if you are a business owner.

Problem-Solving in the Workplace

Most jobs require the ability to solve problems, though not all employees demonstrate that. If you can demonstrate problem-solving skills at your workplace, you increase your chances of moving up in your career and helping your team members. Knowing how to solve problems makes it possible to solve complex problems without a clear solution.

The problem-solving process for the workplace is essentially the same as the problem-solving process described earlier in this chapter:

1. Identify the problem or the premise that needs to be addressed.

2. Gather the facts and form a conclusion.

3. Determine if there is a connection between the problem or premise and the conclusion.

The following is an example:

1. Janet works for a marketing firm. She notices that her client responds better to campaign ideas when her firm incorporates humor. (The identification of the premise).

2. Janet looks back at the past jobs for this client and discovers that the jobs that were approved contained humor while those that lacked humor were not. (Gather the facts and form a conclusion).

3. Janet concludes that she can meet her client's needs by incorporating humor into future projects. (There is a connection between the premise and the conclusion).

How to Develop Your Problem-Solving Skills

The following are suggestions for developing your problem-solving skills:

Strengthen Your Technical Skills

It is easier to solve problems when you have strong technical knowledge of the field in which you are working.

Take Advantage of Opportunity

Look for opportunities in your company where you can be exposed to new situations. You are more likely to find opportunities to problem-solve in such environments. Volunteer to take on a new project or role. If needed, volunteer outside your organization.

Learn from Others

Observe how your coworkers, who are good at problem-solving, handle situations. Talk to them and ask them if they could explain their thinking. Make sure to ask relevant questions so you gain a greater understanding of their methods.

Decision-Making in Business

It is not uncommon for business owners to make important decisions about their business without using logical reasoning. They do not take the time to evaluate an argument's different sides or seek additional information. Instead, they go with their first conclusion or the evidence supporting their beliefs. **The following are three steps for making better business decisions:**

1. Challenge assumptions

2. Use logic

3. Get a diversity of opinions

As you read this, you may say you already do these things. The question is, are you doing them deliberately? The idea is to cultivate these three steps until they become a habit.

Challenge Assumptions

Businesses often make assumptions about their products, services, or customers. Challenging assumptions when dealing with high-state decisions that may affect the business in the long term is important. **Example:**

A business may assume that its product is priced correctly when, in fact, it is overestimating what its customers can afford.

When having discussions with your team, make sure to reply to suggestions with "How do you know___?" **Example:** "How do you know that changing prices will increase sales?" Or you can ask "What if___" questions. Example: "What if we have to change suppliers?" Asking questions like these will help you in your thinking.

Use Logic

When discussing business strategies, it is important that you focus on the logic being used. You want to be sure that every point of the suggested strategy is supported by evidence. Ask yourself if all the evidence leads to a solid conclusion.

An example of this is a company whose major product line has been steadily declining for years, and no one could determine why. This company sold lingerie, and it had decided to go from domestic to international. The problem with the company was that it made the mistake of overgeneralizing. It had assumed that its major product line would appeal to international customers the same way it appeals to U.S. consumers. It had made that assumption based on limited evidence.

If the business owner had challenged the suggestion of going international by asking for evidence to support it, she would have realized that any evidence offered would be weak. Additionally, as previously discussed, it is important to look for any logical fallacies.

Get a Diversity of Opinions

When making major business decisions, it is important to seek out opposing viewpoints. It is normal for people to associate with others who share their mindset. This is especially evident in the online environment. If we only associate with those who agree with us, we become rigid in our thinking.

It is important to go beyond group thinking and seek out other perspectives. Doing so will give you greater insight.

Logical Reasoning in Academics

The philosopher John Dewey was a strong advocate for critical thinking. He believed being a critical thinker was essential in the education system if one was to become an active participant in society. Without critical thinking, Dewey believed students would become passive learners. Critical thinking, he believed, needs to be practiced throughout our lives (Homework Help Global, 2018).

A study by the U.S. Department of Education revealed that the teaching of critical thinking is inconsistent across the nation and decreases as students age. Eighty-six percent of fourth-grade teachers reported teaching critical thinking. The teaching of critical thinking dropped to 50 percent by the time students reached the eighth grade.

Teaching critical thinking in academics is necessary as it allows students to develop new knowledge and information by reflecting on and challenging what they have learned.

Without learning to think critically, students may be able to read well, but they will not comprehend the material. If students cannot think critically, they will not be able to relate or present written ideas logically. Finally, students cannot reason mathematically if they cannot think critically.

The more students develop critical thinking skills, the more they utilize them outside the classroom. This is why critical thinking needs to be incorporated into the classroom. Lessons need to be structured to give students an opportunity for deeper analysis.

CHAPTER 4

Developing Logical Reasoning Skills

Logical reasoning is a soft skill valued in any field of work or study. Fortunately, logical reasoning can be developed at any age. In this chapter, you will find exercises to develop your logical reasoning skills.

Basic Skills

The following exercises involve applying logical reasoning to basic skills:

Logical Reasoning and Reading

Reading is a powerful way to develop logical reasoning skills. When you read, you are gaining knowledge of a specific area. Doing this can stimulate your thinking, leading you to think about other topics. **For this exercise, do the following:**

1. Look in a newspaper for stories that are of interest to you.

2. List the basic premise of each article.

3. Analyze the premises and see if you can identify any relationships or themes.

Logical Reasoning and Writing

The following exercise will help you recognize your strengths and weaknesses, as well as how to make better decisions:

1. Keep a journal to record your daily successes or important moments.

2. Using this information, reflect on past decisions that may have contributed to those

successes or moments. When doing this, consider any errors in your thinking or bad decisions.

3. Analyze your thinking at the time and how it relates to the outcomes you are experiencing today.

Logical Reasoning and Questions

Asking open-ended questions is an excellent way to develop new knowledge and promote personal and professional development. To begin with, let's look at the difference between an open and a closed question. A closed question can be answered by saying "Yes" or "No."

Example:

- "Did you remember the report?"

- "Will you be coming in today?"

- "Are the results consistent with the theory?"

Open-ended questions require a more elaborate answer.

Example:

- "What were the conclusions of the report?"

- "When you come in today, what will you work on?"

- "How can we ensure we are interpreting the results correctly?"

By asking yourself more open-ended questions, you will start to think more critically.

Example:

- What would be the benefits if I choose to_____.

- What would be the shortfalls if I choose to_____?

- What am I not considering in making this decision?

- How would this decision affect me in the long term?

Taking on a New Perspective

How you see yourself and your world is determined by your perspective. If you change your perspective, you change your view of these things. The following exercises will get you to change your perspective, which will challenge your thinking.

The Abilities Exercise

Imagine that you have a disability and you can move only one part of your body. Write about how you believe your life would change from how it is today.

Seek Out Different Perspectives

Develop relationships with people who have different perspectives than you. Try to understand why they see things the way that they do. By doing this, you will expand your perspective, which will help in forming creative solutions.

Who Are You?

This next exercise may be the ultimate existential exercise in critical thinking. Here, you will be challenged by the question posed by philosophers since ancient times: Who are you?

This exercise is so profound because we have based our sense of identity on things such as our name, role, title, or profession. In Buddhist philosophy, it is believed that the "self" is illusionary and does not exist. What will you discover?

Note: It is recommended that you get a pack of index cards to do this exercise.

Using the index cards, write down the qualities that you see yourself as having. **Examples of this are:**

- Enthusiastic

- Honest

- Disciplined

- Dependable

1. Get in a seated position, take a moment to relax, and then mix the cards.

2. Pick one of the cards and reflect on how others (family, friends, coworkers) see you regarding this quality.

   Example: I believe others see me as being honest because of how I_____.

3. Imagine how it would be if that quality did not exist in you. Who would you be without this missing quality? Can you imagine your true self without it? Write down your answer to the best of your ability.

4. Repeat this step with the remaining cards. Be sure to continue writing down your responses with each card.

5. When you are done with the cards, read what you wrote. Can you answer the question, Who are you?

Logical Reasoning and Business

Business owners need to be able to negotiate with internal and external customers and navigate the many challenges of being an employer. The following are exercises for developing the skills needed in these areas.

A Prison in the Neighborhood

1. Imagine that you have been hired to persuade a homeowner's association (HOA) to allow the construction of a new maximum-security prison nearby. This neighborhood is the home of upper-class residents who live in million-dollar homes.

2. **When planning your presentation to the HOA, consider the following:**

a. What benefits would the neighborhood gain from having the prison built there?

b. What incentives could you offer the neighborhood?

3. When answering these questions, you must treat this as a logical reasoning exercise. Your responses need to be logically based, not fantastical thinking.

The Competitors

This exercise is not easy, but if you give it a sincere effort, you may find that you can find creative ideas that benefit your business.

1. Make a list of your business competitors.

2. Next to each competitor, write down what you believe is their purpose for being in business. What are they trying to achieve?

3. When writing down your responses, avoid being judgmental and focus on their purpose.

4. Consider how you could contribute to their success without harming your business.

Suggestions for Strengthening Logical Reasoning Skills

The following are simple suggestions for strengthening your logical reasoning abilities:

Expand Your Skill Set

Make it a point to learn new skills continuously. Do not only learn new skills but practice them daily. By doing this, you will strengthen your logical reasoning capabilities.

Learn from Others

Take time to observe others and how they approach problem-solving. We often get caught up in our problem-solving approach and neglect to learn from others. Learn what strategies they use and how they make decisions.

See the End in Advance

In decision-making, it is important to consider its impact in the long term. How will the decisions you make today impact your future? When making a major decision, try to visualize what the ripple effects will be in the long term. Visualizing future outcomes will strengthen your logical reasoning skills.

Break It Down and Get the Details

Sometimes, we focus on the big picture but miss the details. Before you devise a solution and run with it, please take a moment to break down the situation into its individual components. For example, the simple task of getting ready for your day consists of a variety of other tasks, such as brushing your teeth, taking a shower, getting dressed, having breakfast, and gathering everything you will need to take with you when you leave your home.

Start practicing daily the breaking down of what you do. Doing this will develop a mindset for making important decisions or problem-solving. When making decisions, you can break down the potential consequences of those decisions. When problem-solving, you can break down the elements of the problem. **The following are examples:**

Breaking Down Decisions:

Let's say you need to decide whether to rent an apartment or buy a house. Break down everything involved in renting, and then do the same with buying. When you are done, look at the cost and benefits of each.

Breaking Down a Problem:

If you are an employer with problems retaining employees, you can break down the problem by examining the information. The information being referred to may include interviewing your employees about their feelings about their jobs and reviewing their job descriptions to see if anything needs to be changed.

Conclusion

The importance of logical thinking skills cannot be understated. They play a major role in how we develop in our personal lives and careers. The ability to generate creative ideas and solve problems greatly influences our lives' direction.

Logical reasoning makes it possible to think independently and promotes innovation and creativity. It strengthens analytical thinking and our brains by activating key areas, such as memory. Further, it leads to the strengthening of focus, which helps build self-esteem. Regardless of where you are, it is hoped that you apply what has been presented in this book so that you can become a better version of yourself.

BOOK 4

A Guide to Creative Thinking

What It Is, How to Develop It, and How to Use It

Introduction

Have you ever noticed that there are some people who easily come up with fresh ideas for dealing with situations while others struggle to do the same? Those of us who come up with new ways of approaching things can do so because of creative thinking. Creative thinkers look at situations differently. Because of this, they can come up with unique ways to solve problems.

You do not have to be an artist, musician, or writer to be a creative thinker. Being a creative thinker is not about being one of the "creative" types. Rather, it is about bringing a new perspective to problem-solving, innovation, and managing change. Further, it is a skill that anyone can develop.

By honing your creative thinking abilities, you will be able to tackle life's everyday challenges with a renewed sense of confidence. This will happen because you will be able to find better solutions to your problems as opposed to focusing on your limitations in dealing with situations.

In this book, you will learn how to think differently so that you can develop a skill that will not only change your life but may also change the lives of others.

CHAPTER 1

Foundations of Creative Thinking

Creativity is the ability to perceive things in a new way. It is about coming up with original ideas, recognizing the connections between things, and discovering new solutions. Creativity is not restricted to being artistic. Rather, it is the ability to see life in ways that are often overlooked. Further, creativity can be found within all of us. It is not a situation where some of us are born creative while others lack this ability. The creative muscle is found within all of us; we just need to develop it!

Our lives and the world around us can be shaped by the powerful force of creativity. It strengthens our resilience as it leads not only to finding new solutions but also to new possibilities. Creativity brings about joy and hope by creating greater opportunities for the future, and it helps bring about self-actualization as it allows us to glimpse our greater potential.

Creativity can be inspiring as it can lead to the creation of a marvelous piece of art or an innovative organization. However, creativity also has an important role in everyday life. It enables us to come up with creative solutions to the problems we face on a daily basis. The following are examples of creative thinking:

The Fosbury Flop

Dick Fosbury broke convention at the 1968 Summer Olympics in Mexico City. Fosbury, who competed in track and field, noticed something about the high jumps, which were performed by doing them facing forward. Fosbury discovered that he could gain a greater height by going over backward.

Fosbury's unique jumping style earned him a gold medal, and it changed the sport of high jumping (Schwartz, 2023). Fosbury went against the grain by doing the opposite of what everyone else was doing, a central theme in creative thinking.

Nest

Tony Fadell appeared in the office of Kleiner Perkins to seek investment for his company, Nest. Perkins was familiar with Fadell's involvement in the development of the iPhone and iPod. Perkins was eager to hear Fadell's pitch. To his surprise, Fadell's pitch revolved around redesigning the thermostat!

Past investors were not interested in Fadell's pitch, but Perkins saw something that appealed to him. Fadell told Perkins that he wanted to reimagine the thermostat. It was what Fadell said next that caught Perkins's attention. Besides bringing low-quality videos with him to the pitch, Fadell also brought a block of wood. Fadell continued his pitch by saying that he wanted to "reimagine every unloved product in the home" (Kleiner Perkins, 2014).

Perkins understood Fadell's vision, which the other investors did not get. Fadell wanted to merge the everyday products in our homes with software, turning these "unloved products" into desirable connected devices. Nest would become a dominant player in Silicon Valley, valued at a billion dollars a year. Nest was later bought out by Google.

Understanding Creativity Thinking

As mentioned earlier, creative thinking is the ability to come up with original solutions to problems. Creative thinkers are innovators and natural problem solvers. They ask themselves, "Why?" or "Why not?" rather than accepting the status quo. When faced with a challenge, creative thinkers brainstorm a variety of ideas and then experiment with them to see how they work out in solving the problem.

To better understand creative thinking, let's see what creative thinking looks like in the business environment:

- Conducting an interactive brainstorming session to gather the thoughts of co-workers regarding a project.

- Evaluating a work process and coming up with suggestions on how to make it more effective.

- Looking for alternative ways to market a product and then conducting experiments using new marketing channels.

- Finding original ways to reach out to prospective customers.

- Identifying a new way to promote a brand and coming up with an effective strategy to accomplish this.

Creative thinking can be useful when:

- You have encountered a major challenge, and there is no clear way out of it.

- You are experiencing rapid change and have difficulty seeing where it is leading you. You can then use creative thinking to come up with potential scenarios.

- You find yourself in a situation where there is much disagreement among those around you as to what to do next, and finding a compromise is difficult.

- It is time for new ideas, but you are unsure how to proceed.

Creative Thinking and the Brain

Increased prefrontal cortex activity, as well as activity in other brain regions, is linked to creative thinking. The prefrontal cortex is in charge of several processes that are essential for creative thought, including working memory, planning, and decision-making.

Research studies have demonstrated that certain activities enhance creative thinking. These activities include exercise, being in nature, and meditation. These activities are known to promote relaxation and reduce stress. It is believed that relaxation increases cognitive flexibility, which enhances our ability to problem-solve (Gregory et al., 2013).

Additionally, the research shows that training and practice can enhance our creative abilities. By getting involved in activities that cause you to approach problem-solving in new ways, you can enhance the neural pathways involved in creative thinking (Gregory et al., 2013).

Forms of Creative Thinking

Cultivating creative thinking comes from learning to view life from a different perspective. It is through taking on a different perspective that creative ideas are born. You can change your perspective by practicing innovative thinking. **The forms of innovative thinking are:**

- Divergent Thinking

- Convergent Thinking

- Lateral Thinking

- Aesthetic Thinking

- Inspirational Thinking

Divergent Thinking

Divergent thinking is one of the most common ways of thinking to develop creativity. When using divergent thinking, you come up with a wide variety of ideas without judging or evaluating them. With divergent thinking, you are letting your imagination go wild. An example of divergent thinking is brainstorming.

Divergent thinking is valuable because it frees you from limited thinking and allows you to explore a problem from different angles. Doing this can help identify the problem's root cause. When you have found the root cause, you can use convergent or lateral thinking to find original solutions—ones that you may have never considered before.

Convergent Thinking

Convergent thinking ranks with divergent thinking as the most common type of thinking that is used in coming up with creative solutions. In fact, divergent thinking and convergent thinking often work in tandem with the problem-solving process.

Divergent thinking involves using imagination and coming up with as many ideas as possible.

On the other hand, convergent thinking entails evaluating various concepts to ascertain which one provides the best answer to the issue. By focusing on the most promising solution, you can further develop it to meet your needs.

Lateral Thinking

Lateral thinking involves finding solutions to problems in an unconventional manner. Normally, we engage in logical thinking when problem-solving. With logical thinking, we analyze the situation and come up with the most logical solution.

In lateral thinking, you avoid logical solutions and search for an unconventional solution instead.

Lateral thinking is useful when you are dealing with a challenge or problem where there is no clear approach to take.

You think outside the box and free yourself from any assumptions or boundaries in your thinking. By using this approach, you can find solutions that you never knew existed. The following are examples of lateral thinking in workplace situations:

Customer Service

Many businesses have procedures for handling customers who are demanding or unreasonable. However, sometimes these procedures are ineffective in such situations. In such cases, you could use lateral thinking to provide a better customer experience.

Instead of just giving the customer a refund, you could find another product that would better fit the customer's needs. By doing this, you may leave a better impression on the customer, whereas just issuing a refund may leave the customer with a negative impression of your business.

Running Short on Supplies

Let's say that you are organizing an event for a special situation. Due to shipping issues, you only receive half the decorations you ordered. Using lateral thinking, you could respond to the situation by going to a local store to see if they carry the decorations you need, or you could get creative in the way you place the decorations that you do have.

Aesthetic Thinking

Aesthetic thinking refers to learning to appreciate our perceptions and experiences of life. When engaged in aesthetic thinking, we learn to see and appreciate the beauty that exists within things, or it can involve the other senses, such as the touch, smell, taste, or sound of things.

Aesthetic thinking has real power in our daily lives. From a business perspective, using aesthetic knowledge can be an effective way to reach customers. An example of this is the cosmetic industry. Many cosmetic brands give away free samples. They know that the best way to win customers is to let them have a sensory experience of their product. The customer can see, feel, and smell it.

From a personal perspective, aesthetic thinking means taking time to appreciate the beauty of the extraordinary qualities of those activities that we do routinely and consider to be mundane. You can do this by taking time away from your routine to appreciate those things in your life that you overlook or take for granted.

You can also take time to focus on the emotional and sensory qualities of what you do. For example, you can sit in your garden and pay attention to the emotions it brings out and your sensory experience. What do you see, smell, hear, or feel? By using aesthetic thinking, you are getting in touch with the experience itself rather than glossing over it due to habit or overthinking.

In problem-solving, aesthetic thinking is about reframing the situation so that you can become attuned to its inherent value. For example, you may have an issue with someone with whom you have a relationship. Because your experience with this person has become routine, you may overlook the value they provide to the relationship. Instead, your focus is on the issue. By taking time to appreciate the benefits of being with this person, you may find that the issue involved is less important than you first thought.

Inspirational Thinking

The Beatles' Paul McCartney recounted how he came up with the song "Yesterday," one of the group's most famous songs (Jorlen, 2020). McCartney described how, one morning, he woke up with the tune in his head. He said that he was unfamiliar with the tune and could not understand where it came from.

He went to his piano, where he laid out the chords for the song. He then played it for some of his friends, asking for feedback. McCartney concluded that the song must have come from a dream. McCartney's writing of "Yesterday" is an example of inspirational thinking. Inspirational thinking is creativity that appears to come from a source other than us. It often arises from altered states or dreams.

Those who experience inspirational thinking believe that they have become the conduit for receiving ideas from something or someone else. For this reason, inspirational thinking may be a form of channeling.

Inspirational thinking is often characterized as the receiving of a revelation that contains great clarity and focus and occurs in rapid bursts.

Why You Should Learn to Think Creatively

We tend to go through life caught up in our thinking patterns. In other words, we use the same style of thinking most of the time. That we do so is not by accident, and it has to do with how our brains work. If we spent time analyzing every situation that arose, we would become overwhelmed.

To make our thinking more effective, our brains take shortcuts. Our brains have a habit of overlooking a lot of the information that they take in so that we can make decisions quickly without using up a lot of mental energy.

The problem is that we tend to get stuck in this style of thinking. In doing so, we limit ourselves in that we do not utilize our inherent potential to come up with original and unique ideas that come from creative thinking.

The Benefits of Creative Thinking

Creative thinking is a soft skill that is highly prized by employers. Plus, it offers amazing benefits for your personal life because it gets you to question your assumptions and consider different perspectives, and it helps you stay mentally alert. **The following are additional benefits of learning to think creatively:**

- Creative thinking adds value not only to your life but also to the lives of those around you. Your new ideas can take the form of amazing works that can have a positive impact on the world.

- Creative thinking builds self-reliance and increases confidence as you can come up with solutions on your own without depending on others.

- Creative thinking involves coming up with ideas without judging them. By accepting these ideas, you become less affected by the judgments of others. In other words, you become true to who you are.

- Creative thinking brings excitement to life and gives it greater meaning as you can explore new ideas each day.

- Creative thinking brings out talents that you may not know you have. Then, instead of getting aggravated by problems, you see them as potentially new opportunities.

- Creative thinking causes you to think outside the box, which brings about great satisfaction because you are constantly getting the opportunity to take on new challenges.

- Creative thinking brings with it a great deal of freedom because you feel free to express your feelings. You feel free to be who you want to be at any moment.

- The more you apply creative thinking, the easier it becomes to do, which is invaluable in that you learn to master problematic situations that you face in life.

Creative Thinking versus Critical Thinking

While creative thinking is about coming up with new ideas, critical thinking is more structured and is used to analyze and evaluate information, with convergent thinking being an example of this. When used together, creative thinking and critical thinking are invaluable for arriving at unique solutions.

In the next chapter, we will explore the creative process, where you will find some suggestions for tapping into your creative mind.

Chapter 2

The Creative Process

What is it that makes it possible for some individuals to come up with amazing ideas while others struggle to find just a hint of creativity? What is behind Paul McCartney's musical genius, Thomas Edison's prolific inventive mind, or Jeff Bezos's business savvy? There has been much research into what causes creative genius; however, definitive answers have yet to be found.

What science has found is that the creative process is both contradictory and complex. Further, creative thinking is nonlinear and chaotic. It has nothing to do with the right or left brain. Rather, the creative process involves the whole brain.

When it comes to creative thinking, there is the involvement of the conscious and subconscious minds. It involves emotions and the brain's processing system. Creative thinking involves all these things working together to allow some to see the world in novel ways and translate their ideas into creations that benefit society in unique ways.

Although the concept of creative thinking remains largely understood, science has made some progress. There is now an understanding of how we can more successfully unleash our creative thinking. This understanding is the result of the work of Graham Wallas, a British social psychologist who studied creative individuals.

Wallas wrote the book *The Art of Thought*, in which he proposed a theory of the creative process. This process involves five subconscious steps that creative people follow. **These steps are as follows:**

- Preparation

- Incubation

- Illumination

- Verification

These steps have some resemblance to cooking:

Step 1: Preparation

This first step involves the gathering of the ingredients that you need to cook your idea. At the external level, this first step involves the gathering of knowledge, information, or materials relating to the problem or project that you are involved in. At an internal level, you are engaging with ideas. The preparation step can also involve brainstorming, where you let your ideas flow.

Step 2: Incubation

At this step, you are taking the information from the previous step and letting it marinate. As you let the information marinate, you form new connections with it and gain a deeper understanding of it. This step is not active or intentional. Rather, your attention is on something other than the problem or project. It is by diverting your focus from the project or problem that allows your subconscious to engage with it. In other words, your subconscious is where the cooking takes place. It is where your idea is being cooked.

Step 3: Illumination

Illumination is when your ideas have been fully cooked in your subconscious and are ready to appear in your conscious mind. These ideas often occur unexpectedly and abruptly. Normally, their appearance arises when you are engaged in an unrelated activity, such as taking a walk or showering. Out of nowhere, you experience a eureka moment where the idea or solution presents itself to you.

Step 4: Verification

In this final step, the mental takes physical form. The idea that arises in Step 3 is expressed as a word on the page, paint on the palette, or a developed business plan. At this step, the idea can be further refined or modified.

However, the creative process is not as orderly as just described, as it does not follow in a linear fashion. Rather, the creative process is more like a path that is full of twists and turns. For example, some may not be able to go from the incubation stage straight to the illumination stage. They may have to revisit the preparation stage and get more information.

Others may take the half-baked route, where they go from the preparation step straight to the verification step, skipping the incubation of their idea. There are models of the creative process that include an extra step, which is evaluation. When this step is included, **the process would be as follows:**

- Preparation

- Incubation

- Illumination

- Evaluation

- Verification

The fourth step of evaluation is used more often when problem-solving. At this step, you would take a critical look at your idea and identify its pros and cons. You may also get feedback from others. If the idea does not meet your needs, you can go back to Steps 1 or 2 and start the process again. **The following is an example of this process:**

Preparation:

I received an offer to write a book on creative thinking. I am knowledgeable about psychology and the concept of consciousness. However, I am not too familiar with the concept of creative thinking. I started doing research on the subject. Though I have done my research, I am left with a lot of information that I really cannot connect with.

Incubation

I call it a day as far as researching the subject goes, and I decide to spend the rest of my time listening to music or watching television. Then I go to bed.

Illumination

The next morning, I take a shower, and ideas and insights start coming to mind. I develop connections between the research and my past experiences. Not only do I develop an understanding of the material, but I can also take the information in a whole new direction using my unique insight.

Verification

I write the book from the perspective of my own understanding and experience.

This chapter outlines what little we know about the creative process. In the next chapter, we will explore what research tells us about how creative thinking is influenced by the way we live.

CHAPTER 3

Factors Influencing Creative Thinking

Research appears to indicate that there are both personal and environmental factors that affect our creative ability, which should be no surprise. We are inseparable from our environment like a raindrop that has returned to the ocean. We directly affect our environment, and our environment affects us. The following are personal and environmental factors that affect creativity.

Personal Factors

Motivation

Research shows that the kind of motivation that is used can either kill or foster creativity. The difference lies in whether the motivation is intrinsic or extrinsic. Extrinsic motivation involves external influences, such as the opinion of others or rewards. **The following are examples of extrinsic motivation:**

- Knowing that your performance will be evaluated or judged by others.

- Being observed while you work.

- Having a contractual agreement where you get paid for doing your work.

- Having limitations set on how you can do your job.

- Being in a situation where you are in competition with others.

- Focusing on how you will be rewarded for doing your job, such as money, fame, or power.

The following are examples of intrinsic motivation:

- Experiencing the work as a personal challenge.

- Finding the work interesting.

- Being involved in work where you are learning new things or developing new skills.

- Finding the work to be personally meaningful.

- Finding a higher purpose in the work that you do.

- Experiencing creative flow is a state where you are totally absorbed by the work. This state is often accompanied by a sense of pleasure.

Whenever extrinsic motivators are in play, creativity suffers. Now, let's compare that to intrinsic motivators. Simply put, intrinsic motivation is motivation that comes from doing what you enjoy. You are doing the work for no other reason than the enjoyment and personal challenge that it brings. There are no external factors involved. When intrinsic motivation is at play, creative thinking is enhanced. To illustrate these dynamics between extrinsic and intrinsic motivation, let's use the following research study by psychologist Teresa Amabile (McGuinness, n.d.).

A group of recognized art experts were invited to view the work of professional artists. What the art experts were unaware of was that the artists' work consisted of a combination of commissioned and noncommissioned works. In other words, half of each artist's works were the result of being paid for by a client, while the other half were the result of the artist doing the work for their own enjoyment. The results of the experiment showed that the art experts overwhelmingly rated the noncommissioned work as being more creative than the commissioned work. (McGuinness, n.d.).

In many ways, the results of these studies are common sense. Think of a time when you engaged in an activity that you love, and there was no pressure or constraints on you. Now, compare that situation to one where you were engaged in an activity where there was some form of external pressure placed on you. Under which circumstance did you produce the work that you were most proud of? Odds are, it was doing the work that you found meaningful and fulfilling without any outside pressure to contend with. The work itself was rewarding. It is in this type of situation that creative thinking is at its best.

Passion

Passion is the emotion that is most responsible for driving creativity. Passion is the emotion that keeps us moving forward despite the frustration or stress that may come along the way. It is passion's intensity that makes it a predictor for the employment of creativity.

For passion to effectively drive our creativity, it is important for us to manage the other emotions that often accompany it. For example, passion can be accompanied by frustration when you encounter challenges. For this reason, to sustain your passion, it is important to use coping techniques when any negative emotions are experienced as well. Things that you can do include taking breaks, reevaluating the situation, or looking for the positive in the situation.

Environmental Factors

There has been a lot of research on how the environment affects our creativity. Many of these studies have focused on the workplace, which is where we will begin with this section.

The Physical Space

Research on the workplace has demonstrated that lighting, temperature, and noise levels can significantly impact how creative we are in problem-solving. The following is a breakdown of the major findings:

Sound

Research shows that ambient noise is the best for creative thinking (Cooper, 2014). The reason for this is believed to be due to how sound affects our ability to concentrate. In a quiet space, it makes it easier to focus but more difficult to think creatively. On the other hand, loud music also makes it difficult for creative thinking (Cooper, 2014).

As mentioned earlier, our brains take shortcuts when processing information so that we can make decisions quickly. Ambient noise makes processing information more difficult. As a result, it causes our brains to adopt a processing style that is more abstract. It is this style of information processing that leads to creative thinking. (Cooper, 2014).

Temperature

A study by Cornell University found that the best temperature for productivity and creativity was 77 degrees Fahrenheit (25 degrees Celsius). Employees were more easily distracted when the temperature was 68 degrees (20 degrees Celsius). Also, they were expending extra energy to keep warm (Cooper, 2014).

Lighting

The purpose of discussing how environmental factors affect creativity is so that you can set up the conditions in your surroundings to optimize your creativity. However, it is important to remember that there are different steps in the creative process (see Chapter 2). This means that different creative process steps may have different requirements to achieve optimal results. The relationship between lighting and creativity is an ideal example of this.

When I had to come up with ideas for this book and how I wanted to approach them, I chose to dim the lights.

Studies show that creative thinking is mostly done when the lights are turned down low. The study concluded that dim lighting makes us feel freer to explore new ideas and take risks. When you have your ideas, you may want to choose a well-lit room as it will be easier to focus on the ideas you came up with (Cooper, 2014).

Connecting With Others

You can affect your creativity levels by aligning with others who share your interests. In other words, you can expand your creativity in a certain area by connecting with others who are creative and share your interests. Associating with such individuals will stimulate your thinking and make it easier to come up with creative ideas.

Though having a personal association with such individuals is preferable, you are not limited to this. You can also benefit by exposing yourself to their work. Your thinking will also be stimulated by reading their books, attending their seminars, or watching their videos.

Cultural Immersion

Researchers have concluded that living abroad results in increased creative thinking (Ayyar, 2015). A series of studies looked at students and workers from various countries who spent time living in the United States and Europe. Of special interest to the researchers were those individuals who immersed themselves in the new culture while maintaining a strong connection to their home country (Ayyar, 2015).

These individuals scored higher in creativity than those who did not immerse themselves. Not only did they score higher, but they also enjoyed greater professional success. The researchers concluded that for these individuals to successfully establish themselves in their new country, they had to learn to balance the expectations and societal rules of their adopted and home countries simultaneously (Ayyar, 2015).

To do this successfully requires the skills associated with creativity, such as flexibility in thinking to deal with complex problems. Their encounters with new experiences forced them to shift their perspective and make new connections. (Ayyar, 2015).

Overcoming Mental Blocks

Mental block is a term used to describe a range of experiences where we have difficulty thinking. It is behind what we sometimes refer to as mental fatigue, writer's block, or brain fog. Whatever the term used, mental blocks make it difficult to think clearly, leading to a loss of drive. Naturally, it also affects our creativity. If not addressed, it can compromise your productivity and feelings of contentment. **The following are the main causes of mental blocks:**

Caught up in Routines

Developing routines is a normal part of life. Routines allow us to accomplish our tasks more efficiently and help organize our lives. However, routines have a serious downside if we get caught up in them.

If we do not take time to break away from our routines every so often, we may lose touch with our creative thinking or our expression of it. Routines cause us to stay within our comfort zones, which prevents creative thinking and expression.

Breaking away from our routines means stepping out of our comfort zones. When this happens, we open ourselves to experiencing flow, inspiration, motivation, and creativity. If you are experiencing mental blocks, step out of your routines and experience life differently.

Lighten Up

When we take things too seriously, that can cause mental blocks. This is especially true in the workplace, where professionalism, conformity, and consistency are often stressed. Try to find a balance where you can meet these expectations while at the same time allowing yourself to lighten up. Doing this will allow you to think more creatively at your job and in your personal life.

Being Out of Shape

If you do not exercise, your muscles will not develop. The same is true with your creativity muscles. If you do not exercise your creativity, they will be flabby. Exercising your creative muscles is just as important as exercising your body. Further, you need to have a creative outlet to exercise your creativity. Think of ways you can exercise your creativity muscles daily by creating outlets for their expression. This may involve artwork, writing, singing, planning, daydreaming, or solving puzzles.

Silence the Critic

A big reason for mental blocks is a fear of being criticized for our ideas. However, this fear does not just extend to criticism by others. Many of us criticize our own thinking! We tell ourselves things like "That is nonsense" or "That would never work" when we develop a novel idea.

In criticizing ourselves, we prevent our ideas from fully expressing themselves and provide no opportunity to evaluate them. This can occur not only on an individual level but also on a collective one. If you are part of a work team experiencing mental blocks, you can help alleviate the blockages by encouraging brainstorming meetings where all ideas are encouraged.

Being Burned Out

Burnout occurs when we are constantly overwhelmed by a situation. Burnout saps our energy, which leads to mental blocks and the loss of creativity. It feels like we do not have the energy to move forward at work or in our personal life. **If you are experiencing burnout, the following may be helpful to get you back on track:**

- Create new daily routines that focus on work-life balance.

- Practice mindfulness exercises or meditation.

- Start an exercise routine and stick to it.

- Take time for relaxation and self-care.

- Eat healthfully and get enough sleep.

Lack of Clear Communication

This item refers mainly to work teams where there are challenges with creativity blocks. When a whole team is affected, it is likely due to a communication breakdown. When there is a breakdown in communication, tension among team members is bound to occur. The result is a breakdown in creative thinking. Before mental or creative blocks can be addressed, the issues creating the breakdown in communication need to be addressed first.

Fear of Looking Bad

As with the previous item, this one is common in team settings. Because we do not want to look bad in the eyes of others, we may hold back from expressing our ideas out of fear of being judged or criticized. This kind of thinking stuns creativity and can eventually lead to mental blocks.

Perfectionist Mindset

Those of us who are high achievers are motivated by our desire to do our best. Those of us who are perfectionists are motivated by fear. Perfectionists tend to have self-esteem issues. Their self-esteem is based on being able to do tasks perfectly, which is an impossible expectation for anyone.

A perfectionist fears that others will judge them for not being good enough. As a result, they are never satisfied with what they do because they feel it needs improvement. If they do not believe that they can do something perfectly, they will not even attempt to try.

This kind of pressure on oneself can lead to mental blocks, hinder creative thinking, and place them in a no-win situation as they set standards for themselves that are impossible to achieve. If you have perfectionist tendencies, try to separate thinking creatively from critiquing the idea. The critiquing and evaluation of the idea can be done later.

But That's Not Me!

This is the ultimate creative mind block that some of us have. We tell ourselves that we are not the creative type. It may be true that you cannot paint, write a poem, or compose music. However, these are just forms of creative expression.

All these expressions of creativity were born from creative thought. While everyone may not be artistic, everyone can think creatively. We all can solve problems or develop ideas to improve a certain situation. It is never too late to start developing your creative thinking.

A Problem with Leadership

There are many workplaces where the teams do not think creatively due to a lack of clarity about what is expected. Unless members at the leadership level communicate to their team members that creativity is welcomed, then the team members will not take the time to think of ways that improvements could be made to their work processes.

The Bottom Line

This section describes various reasons we develop mental blocks, both in our personal and professional lives. However, the reasons given could be summed up in three words: the need for certainty.

The need for certainty is inherent in us all. We all need to have a feeling of certainty in our lives. It is as important to us psychologically as oxygen is to us physically.

If expressing our ideas feels emotionally unsafe, we will not further develop them or share them with others. To overcome mental blocks, we need to give ourselves permission to explore our ideas and encourage others to do the same. If we do this, we transform society by developing certainty that our ideas have value and can contribute to a more advanced society.

CHAPTER 4

Techniques for Enhancing Creative Thinking

As mentioned earlier, the nature and dynamics of creative thinking remain largely misunderstood. Despite this, techniques for developing creative thinking have emerged. In this chapter, we will explore three of these techniques: divergent thinking, convergent thinking, and creative exercises.

Divergent Thinking

Divergent thinking is a form of creative thinking that involves coming up with a wide range of ideas for solving a problem. When using divergent thinking, you want to think outside the box. You want to encourage the free flow of thought without any judgment. The idea is to come up with and explore unique and new perspectives and ways of thinking. You want to challenge the norm and open yourself up to the unconventional. Later, these ideas can be evaluated and narrowed down until you find the best solution.

The following are the characteristics of divergent thinking:

- It is creative in providing the opportunity to arrive at unique ideas that may otherwise not have been considered.

- It is fluid in that it allows the production of many ideas.

- It provides flexibility for coming up with varied ideas for varied topics.

Divergent thinking offers important advantages, which include:

The Generation of New Ideas and Possibilities

Divergent thinking opens your mind and allows you to explore new perspectives. It gets you to challenge the status quo and seek out better answers.

It Develops Creativity

Because divergent thinking gets you to think outside the box, creativity and problem-solving are enhanced, resulting in innovative ideas.

It Results in Better Answers

As divergent thinking encourages the challenging of traditional norms, it can lead to coming up with better answers to problems.

These three advantages all point to the same thing: an aspect of our mind that we often underutilize or are not even aware of. There is an aspect of the mind whose intelligence is more sophisticated than our conscious minds.

When we face a problem or are trying to come up with an idea, we often limit ourselves to the conscious mind, where we mull over the situation as we try to find an answer. This kind of effort uses up a lot of mental energy and can lead to mental blocks. A more effective way is to allow that part of the mind to do the work for us.

I remember when I had a challenge I was dealing with, and there were no clear answers. I went to a park and took a moment to ask myself, "What would be the best response to this problem?" I then forgot about the situation as I took a stroll.

My mind was on the beauty of my surroundings, not my problem. Sure enough, the answer to my problem came without effort. Instead of worrying about and pondering the problem incessantly, I let my subconscious hijack it. When the answer was ready to be revealed, it came effortlessly. **The following are techniques that you can use to activate your divergent thinking:**

Brainstorming

Brainstorming is a technique that can be used individually or as a group. The idea behind brainstorming is to develop as many ideas as possible in a short period of time, say five minutes. Whether you are doing it individually or as a group, it is important not to judge any ideas. The goal of this technique is to get the ideas out there! By expressing ideas freely, you get into a flow where unique ideas can surface.

Mind Mapping

With mind mapping, you visually represent the ideas and concepts you are working on. By diagraming the ideas and concepts, you can see their relationship, which can lead to new insights and connections.

Freewriting

Freewriting is a good technique when you need to focus on a single subject. Choose a specific time when you will dedicate yourself to writing about the subject. When writing, do not worry about neatness, grammar, or spelling. Your only job is to get your thoughts on paper. As with brainstorming, let your thoughts flow and get them down on paper. At another time, you can go back to it and restructure or organize your writing if needed.

Convergent Thinking

While divergent thinking is about getting into a thought stream and letting it flow, convergent thinking involves taking those ideas and evaluating them for the best possible answer.

Convergent thinking is most effective when you have evaluated the information and need to choose an answer. It involves considering the different possibilities and evaluating them against the known information. Doing so involves rational thinking, reasoning, and then deciding.

This contrasts with divergent thinking, which is most effective when facing a problem but has no clear answers. For these reasons, an effective way to solve problems is to use divergent thinking in conjunction with convergent thinking. Start with divergent thinking to develop ideas and follow up with convergent thinking to evaluate and select the best solution. **The following are two examples of convergent thinking:**

You are following a wellness plan to become healthier. When determining what you will eat for breakfast, you consider that yesterday you had an intense workout. You also joined friends for a celebratory lunch where you ate a lot of pizza. Thinking convergently, you decide to have a protein drink for breakfast. It meets your nutritional needs, and it is healthy.

Here is a second example: You are a project leader who must deal with important decisions with far-reaching implications. Further, you need to make decisions quickly. To do this, you must consider everything known about the situation, organize the information, analyze it, and then choose the best answer.

Convergent Thinking Techniques

The following are various techniques that promote convergent thinking:

Grouping

You will wind up with a lot of information when using divergent thinking. Grouping is a technique that employs convergent thinking. By organizing the information in groups, it is easier to narrow down the available information so that it is easier to choose a solution.

Prioritizing

By prioritizing information, you can determine which information is most relevant for choosing a solution and which information can be reviewed later.

Filtering

Filtering is like prioritization in the way you manage information. When dealing with copious amounts of information, it is important to remove information that we do not plan to act on and to focus on the information that appears relevant.

The Good and the Bad of Convergence Thinking

The advantage of convergence thinking is its efficiency. Rather than coming up with new solutions all the time, convergence thinking involves logic and allows you to make decisions quickly. Further, its structured process allows you to leverage methodologies you are familiar with to avoid guesswork.

The disadvantage of convergent thinking is that it leaves no room for creative thinking, so it will not lead you to new ways of thinking or innovative solutions. Further, it does not work well with complex problems. Convergent thinking works well with straightforward problems. If the problem involves multiple variables, convergent thinking can be counterproductive as it does not account for the different variables that may be involved.

Finally, the danger of convergent thinking is that it relies on established information, which may contain cognitive biases and not support diversity or peer learning. Divergent thinking will address these concerns.

The difference between divergent and convergent thinking can be illustrated by how the problem is presented and the questions that are asked:

Divergent Thinking

Your company laptop is not working properly. Further, you have a project due tomorrow by the end of the day. Because you work from home, your company's IT department cannot send you a replacement in time. What can you do to complete your project on time?

Convergent Thinking

Your company laptop is not working properly. Further, you have a project that is due tomorrow by the end of the day. Because you are working from home, your company's IT department cannot send you a replacement in time. What three people have the knowledge and skills to complete the project so that you can find out their availability?

As you can see, the problem was the same for both thinking styles. What changed were the questions that were posed. The convergent style focuses on whom you could delegate the responsibility. The divergent example considers other options, such as finding a local computer repair service to repair your computer or using a different device until you get a replacement laptop from IT.

When Divergent and Convergent Thinking Join Forces

When problem-solving, combining divergent and convergent thinking can provide you with the best solutions because the two thinking styles balance each other out. The positives of both thinking styles will work in your favor, while each style will compensate for the weakness of the other. **The following are examples of this:**

Creating a Pricing Strategy

An entrepreneur is trying to determine the price of their product. They need to meet their bottom line and earn a profit. To do this, they need to rely on math and the projections of the market. Using convergent thinking, they can determine their production costs. They can then use divergent thinking to develop various pricing scenarios and experiment with various pricing strategies to meet their sales goals.

Product Maintenance

The owner of a software company needs to perform maintenance on her software product and develop new features. Her team will use convergent thinking to optimize the coding and fix bugs, as these tasks require a systematic approach. Her team will use divergent thinking when introducing new features or experimenting with new technology.

Identifying a Problem's Root Cause

Imagine that you are a business owner. You realize that your marketing plan is not resulting in your projected sales. You could use divergent thinking to examine the issue from different perspectives, such as faulty messaging, the wrong target audience, or technical problems.

Having developed these different perspectives, you can use convergent thinking to do a more targeted analysis and use your knowledge of previous successful campaigns to help inform the direction you take.

Creative Exercises

When we hear the words "creative exercises," we may think about the arts, such as dance, painting, and design. However, creative exercises in this book refer to improving overall creativity, which includes coming up with new ideas and problem-solving.

Creative exercises are also useful for improving the creative thinking of work teams and are used by forward-looking businesses. In this context, creative exercises can improve group creativity and cohesion. **The following are some of the benefits of creative exercises:**

- Improved mental flexibility, allowing you to notice changes that you previously overlooked.

- Increase your ability to find new solutions to repetitive problems.

- Develop a more positive attitude toward work challenges by seeing them as an opportunity to test your mental creativity.

- Improve teamwork skills such as problem-solving and communication.

Suggestions for Creative Exercises

The following are examples of creative exercises. Many of these exercises are considered group activities, but **they can be modified for individual use:**

Incomplete Figure Challenge

The incomplete figure test involves creating a complete drawing from a simple scribble. Start by making a small scribble, such as a loop or half circle. Using the scribble, draw a complete drawing.

The Paper Clip Challenge

A mental exercise, the paper clip challenge involves using your imagination to think of many ways that paper clips can be used other than holding pages together. In a group setting, members can share their ideas.

The Music Challenge

Play music at your workplace. While listening to the music, write down any ideas that come to you. When you finish writing down your ideas, see if they are relevant to any work issues you may be experiencing.

The Dictionary Story

Select a random word from the dictionary. Upon selecting a word, take note of the word that appears above it and the word below it. Using these three words, write a short but cohesive story. This exercise is good for improving our ability to make connections between ideas that may not appear to relate to each other.

Compound Collaborative

Think of a compound word, such as "butternut," and replace one of the words with another (example: "applenut"). Write a story or make a drawing of your new compound word. This exercise will help you find connections between seemingly unrelated objects.

Your Day as a Poem

Write a poem that depicts how your day is going. If applicable, write it in the style of a poet you admire or structure it as a classic poem, such as a haiku or sonnet. Writing in a structured format will force you to find the ideal phrase or words to conform to the constraints of the structure.

Progressive Drawing

Pick an object and draw it every day for a week. Each time you draw the object, see if you can pick up details or nuances you overlooked the day before. This exercise will get you to focus more and pay closer attention to details.

Free Writing

Every morning, take time to write freely without any intentions. Allow yourself to enter a stream of consciousness and write down your thoughts. When doing this exercise, writing nonstop without thinking about it is important. Let your ideas come to you. This exercise can bring about creative solutions to workplace challenges.

SCAMPER

SCAMPER is a brainstorming method that teams can employ to develop or innovate their services or products. **SCAMPER stands for:**

- Substitute

- Combine

- Adapt

- Modify/Magnify

- Purpose

- Eliminate/Minimize

- Rearrange/Reverse

Substitute

Regarding the service or product, what could be replaced? Things to consider are materials, components, or people.

Example: If you manufacture aquariums, could you replace the glass with acrylic for durability and safety?

Combine

Could you combine the product or service with other features?

Example: Most cell phones have the combined features of a phone and a camera.

Adapt

What could be added to the product or service?

Example: Most cars nowadays come with Wi-Fi.

Modify

What aspects of the product or service could be maximized, minimized, or modified in other ways? Could the shape, size, or color be changed?

Example: Changing the color of a children's toy to make it more attractive to them.

Purpose

Could the product or service serve a different purpose or be used by a different industry?

Example: During the COVID-19 pandemic, coffee filters were used as added protection in face masks.

Eliminate

What part of the product or service could be removed?

For example, LinkedIn removed its Stories feature because users were uninterested.

Reverse

What parts of the product or service can be reversed, rearranged, or re-engineered?

Example: Fast food restaurants reversed the traditional eat and then pay model of restaurants to pay and then eat.

When SCAMPER is used in the workplace, it can be helpful to have a warm-up game where you present the teams with random objects, such as a paperclip or hat, and have them apply the SCAMPER method to it before using it on the product or service.

Creativity can be applied to any area of life. In the next chapter, we take a brief look at the application of creativity as well as prospects for its use.

CHAPTER 5

Creative Thinking in Different Fields

Creativity is a quality that exists within us all. Its expression goes beyond artistic talent; it can be expressed in any endeavor we undertake. Also, creativity is the foundation of innovation. In this chapter, we will explore the role of innovation in business, education, and creativity in personal development.

Innovation and Business

The term "innovation" is often connected to technology. However, innovation is a real aspect of business. In business terms, innovation implies the driving of revenue. But what is at the heart of innovation? The answer is creativity and adaptability.

Business innovation involves implementing new ideas, services, products, or processes to boost the bottom line. It does not involve inventing. Innovation is vital in business to keep up with changes in the marketplace.

The Benefits of Business Innovation

Four primary benefits result from business innovation:

Staying Ahead of the Curve

If properly conducted, business innovation responds effectively to potential disruptions or changes in consumer demands. Businesses can utilize information from these events and undertake strategic changes. **Examples of such changes can include:**

- Creating new services or products that are like startups are offering.

- Purchasing products from others in the industry.

- Forming partnerships with upstarts.

Improved Efficiency

Business innovation can also take place by making current processes more efficient. By making changes to processes, businesses can save time and money, allowing them to adapt to industry shifts.

Attraction and Retention

Innovations that will attract and retain employees are important, especially among millennials and Gen Z, who are looking for fast-moving and mission-driven businesses.

Brand Perception

Today's consumers prefer to purchase from businesses they believe to be socially conscious and innovative.

Examples of Business Innovation

The following are examples of business innovation in a variety of industries:

GE Healthcare

GE Healthcare became aware of the problems that healthcare providers encounter when using their diagnostic imaging products with pediatric patients. Many children became upset by the darkness of the room, the flickering lights, and the long procedures.

After speaking to medical staff and industry experts, GE used the insights that they gained to create child-friendly magnetic resonance imaging machines. One such machine, Pirate Adventure, resembles a pirate ship surrounded by images of sandcastles, beaches, and oceans. These innovations made the children happier, improved the quality of pediatric scans, and saved consumers time and money.

Oral-B

The story of Oral-B demonstrates the importance of testing out initiatives before implementing them. Oral-B hired designers to give their electric toothbrushes an upgrade. Oral-B wanted to add functions to their toothbrush that would allow users to track their brushing frequency, play music, and be gentler on sensitive gums.

The designers pointed out to Oral-B that users did not care for these additional functions. Instead, consumers wanted a better experience. Oral-B listened to the feedback and developed a new idea that made their product more convenient for users. The innovation was making the ordering replacement heads by consumers simpler by designing the toothbrush so that it could connect to a cellphone, allowing the sending of reminder notifications to Oral-B.

Netflix

Several times, Netflix used innovation successfully and on a large scale. The first was when the company switched over to a subscription delivery service. Before the switch, Netflix used the same model as Blockbuster, its primary competitor. This model required the customer to drive to the store to select a video and then drive back to return it.

The next major innovation came when Netflix understood that DVDs were becoming obsolete. In response, the company switched to becoming an on-demand streaming service.

Creativity in Education and Learning

As in the business sector, innovation is vital in education, especially now. Unlike the business sector, education has largely lagged in innovation, with teaching methods remaining the status quo. The result is a growing gap between the skills needed in the marketplace and how students are taught.

The goal of education is to prepare students to advance in their education or training to succeed in their career goals and give back to society. However, a study of job preparedness revealed that 64 percent of hiring managers felt their employees struggled to keep up with evolving skill requirements. In comparison, 70 percent of hiring managers felt that their employees had yet to master the needed skills (Thompson, 2022). The Program for International Student Assessment (PSA) also found that the United States ranked 13th out of 79 countries for reading levels and 37th for math (OECD, 2019).

Innovation in education parallels that in business. It is an openness to look at current problems from a fresh perspective and find innovative ways to change them. Innovation is a process, not an outcome. It means the willingness to improve knowledge transfer using new approaches, even if we do not know all the answers. **The following are examples of innovation in education:**

- Project-based learning is where students learn to identify real-world problems and find solutions. In addition, project-based learning provides opportunities for creative thinking and collaboration.

- Incorporate blended learning where online and traditional classroom learning are combined. Blended learning allows students to learn how to best use the tools they will use in their work environment.

- Provide improved communication methods between the school district and parents by incorporating effective video tools.

The following are examples of schools that have innovated the learning experience:

The Urban Cottage Educational Collaborative

The Urban Cottage Educational Collaborative was started in 2015 in Tampa, Florida. It provides a unique learning environment by providing students with a variety of services, **including:**

- Small group classes for schooled students

- After-school programs for students attending traditional school settings

- Summer camps

Urban Cottage was created in recognition of the fact that no one structure can fit the needs of every child or family. In addition, it gives its instructors the freedom to customize their lessons for students.

AIM Educational Collaborative

In Wichita, Kansas, AIM Educational Collaborative was founded by Dalena Wallace, who homeschooled her children. Years later, she expanded her role by becoming the manager of a homeschool cooperative. The cooperative comprised homeschooling families working together to share classes, activities, and other resources. That effort grew to become a micro-school (a school limited to fifteen students) and a hybrid homeschool (students attend traditional classes part of the week and work from home the rest of the days). These options are part of the AIM organization, which serves families by offering them the best option that works for them.

Ideas for Improving Education

Urban Cottage and AIM are just two examples of how concerned parents worked to improve education. We are undergoing a technological revolution that, if adopted by the educational system, could lead to the revolutionizing of the educational experience.

Artificial Intelligence (AI)

AI, such as ChatGPT, can be used to draft essays, book reports, and more. Some are critical of using ChatGPT in the classroom out of fear that students will become too reliant on it. However, educators have found workarounds where ChatGPT can be used while requiring students to demonstrate independent knowledge and ability, such as in-person writing assignments and exams. At the same time, students could learn how to use AI and its limitations.

A study of over 2,000 K-12 educators revealed that over half were using ChatGPT, and 10 percent were using it daily. Further, 88 percent of educators and 79 percent of students had positive opinions of its use in the educational setting (Walton Family Foundation, 2023).

Virtual Reality

Virtual reality could transform education by creating interactive and immersive student learning experiences. They could participate in simulations that would be difficult or impossible to replicate anywhere else. Students could go back in time, experience historical events, or travel in space.

The use of virtual reality provides the opportunity for problem-solving under controlled and safe conditions while developing a greater understanding of complex concepts. Though only 15 percent of the U.S. population utilizes virtual reality, a recent study indicated that 93 percent of educators and 93 percent of students believed that virtual reality would positively impact the educational experience (Kolmar, 2023).

Creativity and Personal Development

As mentioned earlier, creativity goes beyond being artistic. Creativity goes beyond being able to write, create music, or paint. You can think of creativity as an aspect of intelligence, and it expresses itself in each person differently. Instead of being able to compose a song, perhaps you are good at problem-solving. Instead of writing a screenplay, perhaps you can easily connect with others and favorably influence them.

Regardless of how you express your creativity, you can enhance it by using it. In this way, creativity is like a muscle. We all have it, but its level of development varies from person to person.

Creativity and Personal Growth

The essence of creativity is self-expression. Creativity is the act of sharing an aspect of ourselves with others. In this manner, creativity is like a bridge that connects us to the inner and outer realms.

Through creativity, we can explore our inner realm, the realm of thoughts and feelings, and communicate them to the world and ourselves. It is this communication that leads to personal growth. The personal growth indicated here can express itself in innumerable ways. However, some of the more basic ways include critical thinking skills, problem-solving, and adapting to changing situations.

Benefits of Creative Expression

The benefits of creative expression are vast in number. The following are just a few of them:

Endorphin Release

Engaging in creative pursuits releases the feel-good hormone endorphins. Endorphins create a sense of well-being by reducing stress levels (Babiedaite, 2023).

Mental and Emotional Health

Creative expression comes about by processing our thoughts, emotions, and experiences. Doing this creates a sense of perspective and greater self-awareness, all of which contribute to mental and emotional well-being (Babiedaite, 2023).

Self-Knowledge

To think creatively is to engage in self-discovery. It brings about a greater understanding of ourselves and our place in the world while developing the critical thinking and problem-solving skills needed to navigate it.

For these reasons alone, expressing the creative aspect of yourself throughout your life keeps you on an endless journey of discovery.

Conclusion

It is my belief that we live in an intelligent universe whose undefinable intelligence permeates all of existence. We are the recipients of this creative energy, and it flows through all of us. The challenges that we face as a species can, without question, be addressed using this creativity. My wish is that you develop your creativity and use it, whether it is on a global scale or in your personal life, to create value for yourself and those around you. When creativity is guided by wisdom, there is no challenge that we cannot overcome.

Thank You

Before you leave, I'd just like to say, thank you so much for purchasing my book.

I spent many days and nights working on this book so I could finally put this in your hands.

So, before you leave, I'd like to ask you a small favor.

Would you please consider posting a review on the platform? Your reviews are one of the best ways to support indie authors like me, and every review counts.

Your feedback will allow me to continue writing books just like this one, so let me know if you enjoyed it and why. I read every review and I would love to hear from you.